CHARLES MORGAN was born in Kent in 1894. He was educated from boyhood as a naval officer, and served in the Atlantic and China fleets before the First World War. In 1913 he left the Navy to become a writer; but August, 1914, found him back in the service. He went to the front with the Naval Brigades in October, took part in the defense of Antwerp, and was a prisoner of war for four years. That Dutch interlude gave him the background for "The Fountain."

After the war he went to Oxford, where he took Honours in Modern History and was President of the Dramatic Society. In 1921 he joined the editorial staff of the *Times* (of London); and from 1926 until the outbreak of the present war he was principal dramatic critic to that newspaper. Meanwhile his novels began to appear. "Portrait in a Mirror" (1929) founded a reputation which "The Fountain" established and "Sparkenbroke" confirmed in England, the United States, and throughout Europe. Mr. Morgan is the only author to whom the Femina Prize, the Hawthornden Prize, and the James Tait Black Memorial Award, all three, have been given, and is one of the few Englishmen to receive the Légion d'Honneur for literary work. Apart from novels, he has written "Epitaph to George Moore" and a play—"The Flashing Stream." His books have appeared in fourteen languages.

At the beginning of the present war Mr. Morgan served in the Admiralty for a period; then, during the summer of 1940, he completed "The Voyage," a love story of France in the eighties, which was followed by "The Empty Room," a story set in present-day England. Macmillan & Company, Ltd., commissioned him to write its centennial history —published in 1943 as "The House of Macmillan"; and this is now followed by the present book, "Reflections in a Mirror."

REFLECTIONS IN A MIRROR

BY

CHARLES MORGAN

NEW YORK
THE MACMILLAN COMPANY
1945

Copyright, 1945, by
CHARLES MORGAN

FIRST PRINTING

A WARTIME BOOK

*This complete edition is produced in full
compliance with the government's regulations for conserving paper and other
essential materials.*

PRINTED IN THE UNITED STATES OF AMERICA

FOREWORD

THE idea underlying these essays is, I hope, made clear in the first of them, " In Search of Values ". One, " Emily Brontë ", has already been published in a volume called " The Great Victorians ", edited by H. J. and Hugh Massingham and published by Nicholson and Watson, to whom I express my thanks. The others have not been included in a book until now. They are selected from a weekly series, " Menander's Mirror ", which began to appear in the *Literary Supplement* of *The Times* on October 31st, 1942.

To the editors of *The Times* and of the *Supplement*, I owe more than formal gratitude. Other work arising from the war having deprived me of leisure in which to found a novel, I had come to feel that I might never write again. At this bleak moment, *The Times*, from which, after long association, the war had separated me on September 1st, 1939, invited me to undertake the Menander essays, and, though the pressure on space can never have been more severe, put a page of the *Supplement* at my disposal. Having granted me a free hand in the choice of subject, the paper afterwards intervened only to give encouragement. No greater kindness can be done to a writer.

The essays in the present book have been chosen, not necessarily because I prefer them to others that have been reserved, but to represent the series as far as the limitations of a single volume allow. I have not arranged them in categories, for the reader may prefer to find variety in each group of four or five. They have been carefully revised, but changed scarcely at all except to ease a sentence here and there by readmitting the pronoun " I ", which the tradition of the *Supplement* excludes.

C. M.

CONTENTS

	PAGE
IN SEARCH OF VALUES . . .	1
ON BEING BORN NOW . . .	9
THE INTEGRITY OF PASCAL . .	18
THE RETURN OF FRANCE . .	26
THE IDEA OF EUROPE . . .	34
A LEISURED CIVILIZATION . .	43
WHY BIRDS SING	51
THE HERITAGE OF SYMBOLISM .	60
ON PICKING SIDES . . .	68
ON BEING A PRISONER . . .	77
" LA DOUCEUR DE VIVRE " . .	86
THOMAS HARDY	95
AN EXPECTANT SILENCE . .	112
THE ABBEY	121
EMILY BRONTË	130
THE UNCOMMON MAN . . .	147
ITALIA IRREDENTA . . .	156
IVAN TURGENEV	165
NAUSICAA AND THE PELICANS .	174
THE MIGHTY STRONG BEAST . .	183
TOLSTOY : " WAR AND PEACE " .	192
TOLSTOY : THE SECOND EPILOGUE .	201
ON UNRELATED KNOWLEDGE . .	217

In Search of Values

OF all contemporary catchwords, the most frequent and insidious is this : " Nothing will ever be the same again ; the old world is gone ". When it is said with regret, the speaker is reproved for the now unfashionable vice of nostalgia, but when it is spoken in the complacent tone of an adolescent who has thieved his father's latchkey, it is often endorsed and applauded. The nostalgic use of it is the less harmful, for except in rarely imaginative instances the young are proof against their parents' regrets. It becomes dangerous only when they who are themselves young and have a right to look forward believe it to be true and try to build their house on that sandy and shifting lie.

Those who cheerfully utter it — and Ministers of the Crown are not guiltless — appear to believe that they are realists, " facing the facts " and stimulating their audience to constructive endeavour. A little reflection shows that they are nothing of the kind. They are dazzled future-gazers, the converse cousins of that Colonel Blimp who has become a symbol of fatuous conservatism. As he looks back, so they look forward, without discernment, without attempt to distinguish between what is " gone " for better and what for worse, and without noticing or even remembering those elements of the past that are indestructible. Art is not " gone ", nor love, nor belief in God. These, as Russia has re-proved, have a habit of surviving revolutions, and not these only but lesser human loyalties and faiths. If one is thinking in terms of particular privileges or graces, even if one is thinking, more broadly, in terms of a material way of life, it is at least not unreasonable, though still highly disputable, to say that they are " gone ", but wisdom did not perish when the library at Alexandria was destroyed, Hellenism did not die when Athens fell, and it is unreasonable to suggest that those who survive the present historical episode will find themselves miraculously exempt from the embarrassments, and deprived of the glories, of our history and character.

This is not simply to repeat the truism that the word " new " is always a lie ; it is, rather, to indicate that what genuinely concerns us is much less to make generalized contrasts between historical periods than to estimate the ever-changing friction between what is essential and continuous and what is variable in the development of society. The difficulty always is to prevent our own prejudices from assigning permanence to what is ephemeral or, if our vice happens to be " the craven fear of being thought illiberal ", to avoid the opposite error of supposing that nothing in human nature can defy our earnest reforms. The Blimps say roundly that you cannot change human nature, and, on that plea, immobilize their thought ; the future-gazers are so dazzled by the changing spots that they forget the leopard. The middle truth appears to be that in all societies and at all times there are both constants and variables, and that what gives to an age its distinguishing character is the relationship, the friction, between them.

This friction may be discerned in every aspect of life. Art is continuous in the sense that man's desire to hold a mirror up to nature is continuous, but the angle at which he holds the mirror and the point of view from which he regards it vary from decade to decade. A corresponding change is to be observed in his attitude towards that complex of desire and fear, of hunger and aspiration, which is called love. Here, too, there are constants and variables — an abiding sensual instinct, for example, and varying refinements or sublimations of it — which, by their interactions, produce, upon the visible surface of society, an "emancipation of women" or a "romantic revival" or what you will. So, also, man's religious intuition is continuous; only the degree and manner of his submission to it are variable. In this, as in all else, those who announce that nothing will be the same again because another group of barbarians has temporarily overrun Europe are taking only the variables into account. In their estimate of change, in their measure of things to come, they omit two considerations : first, the constants ; second, the understanding that what is effective to change society is not the variables themselves but the tensions set up between the variables and the constants. These tensions are the proper study of criticism that seeks to penetrate a little below the appearances of things.

If, in the field of art, the tension changes ; if it slackens ; if the angle at which man holds his mirror up to nature becomes increasingly oblique; if, under the influence of war, he exalts the value of power or the value of self-preservation, then his aesthetic value falls in his scale of values ; and the rise or fall of this, as indeed of any, value is remarkable not only in itself but because it implies a shifting and, in the end, perhaps, a reorganization of the whole scale. Man cannot begin to think less of art without, at the same time, beginning to think more, or less, of religion, of love, of equality, of possessions, of power, of all else by which his mind and spirit are engaged. The values are interdependent, and it is the duty of criticism which is to be something else than an impression of one book, one picture or one play, of aesthetic criticism, that is to say, which is also a criticism of life, to be alive to this interdependence.

3

In it there may, perhaps, be found a present consolation which has nothing to do with the vague optimism that is part of the future-gazers' stock-in-trade. To pretend, as they do, that it is immoral or cowardly to look back with longing to certain elements of the past and to hope for the preservation of some of them is to pretend a lie. What gives colour to their lie is that the English, great and small, are now deeply persuaded that they must cut their losses and, not without sorrow but still without fear or bitterness, are adapting their minds to radical change. What shakes them, what shakes us all sometimes, is a sense of illimitable landslide, of the ground itself dissolving under our feet — a nightmare-feeling that what may be required of us is to awake in a world altogether unrecognizable. The future-gazers' irresponsible optimism is no reassurance. The only corrective to that black mood is to observe for ourselves the evidences of strength in our civilization and to observe them far and wide — in the fact, for example, that, among a spate of propaganda, selfless and scholarly books are still published and read, or in the proofs which reach us in increasing strength that in France, in Scandinavia, in all the occupied territories, desire for the reintegration of a free Europe is burning and effective. In making these observations it is our duty to draw clear distinguishing lines between what seems good to us personally, because it flatters our wish or annoys our opponents, and what is, in truth, a value to be fought for, not only for its own sake but as part of a spiritual landscape which, we are determined, shall not be " altogether unrecognizable " when all is done. Criticism, in other words, is having a new coherence forced upon it.

Twenty-five years ago men were filled with extravagant hopes of vast political rewards for their suffering. They placed so great a reliance on a political reorganization of Europe that, when Geneva became no more than a shadow of their hopes, they fell into that mood of " disenchantment " which C. E. Montague described. To-day, if one may put it so, the investment of man's hope in the future is more widely spread. It is investment for an income, not for a gambler's rise, and a great part of the income will, we know, come from sources within ourselves — from our power to become genuinely detached from a thousand pleasant vanities, and from the strength with which, in the face of all popular clamour, we stand by and develop what remains. And there seems to be arising among the English a power to distinguish, to see things in perspective, such as they have never before possessed. The commentators, noticing a change but not perceiving its nature, have been surprised by it. Why no marching songs ? Why, even among civilians, none of the wildly expressed hatreds of a quarter of a century ago ? Why so conspicuous an absence of the romantic spark ? The reason is by no means hopelessness or indifference, but a desire for proportion, a will to distinguish the first things, to put them first, and the rest in order. This determination was evident before Pearl Harbour in the almost complete understanding in England of the American point of view, and has been plain since 1940, even among those who have no emotional bias towards France, in the balance of the English attitude towards the French. It is as if the whole nation were patiently striving to prevent any kind of false emphasis now from making impossible a steady reordering of their values. From whatever angle we regard the human scene, we shall think vainly, and against the wisdom of the age, if we allow our sense of their interdependence to be dulled.

These essays will fall short of their purpose if this sense of a vital interdependence of values is not preserved and communicated in them. Their range is wide. A reader who comes upon one by chance may see in it only a discussion of a particular subject and may for that reason be the better entertained ; but there is nevertheless a free relationship between them, which will, I hope, appear gradually, as it might in the continued conversations of friends. In discussing the rise or decline in public favour of an author or an idea, I have tried not only to note the fact and comment on it, but to inquire how much of the change is to be dismissed as a swerve of fashion, and how much of it is more deeply significant as a pointer to an enduring change of values. If the essays are concerned with literature, they avoid the coteries like the plague ; if with war, they are innocent of strategy ; if with social problems, they are at any rate not an arsenal for any party. That prejudice will be found in them is certain and even desirable, provided that the writer admits, as he does most freely, that his, like all opinion, is, in part, emotional ; only when a man asks us to believe that his admiration of his mistress's eyebrow is the product of pure reason does his prejudice become a lie and he a bore. Finally, these papers ask more questions than they presume to answer. They put forward the speculative inquiries of a man whose claim to make them is, precisely, that he is fallible and that his freedom from a prophet's robes may recommend him to argument — but of a man, it should be added, who is himself too deeply moved by the tragedies and the expectations of contemporary life to forbear from asking questions that strike into the hearts of controversy or from struggling towards the truth where he sees a glimmer of it. The reader will not be able to give his answers sentence by sentence, but he may well think of himself, not as listening to a discourse, but as taking part in a series of dialogues.

Much of a dialogue's spirit depends upon its scene

and the reader will choose that which seems best to him. We all have our own ways, dating from childhood, of by-passing our authors' descriptive passages ; our biblical scenes are laid in the first house or the first garden we knew, and Alice, to this day, steadily pursues her adventures in our own wonderland. It would, therefore, be foolish to insist that these discussions have a particular setting ; the reader's mood and habit will override any stage directions ; but it may not be meaningless, even to a reader in South Carolina or Connecticut, to suggest that they have their meditative origin in St. James's Park — a pleasant territory of trees, islands and calm water where formerly men and women idled and where now they march to work. Here every morning, between Buckingham Palace and Whitehall, beside the lake or across the enchanted bridge that looks out over Corot's water to the Foreign Office, men and women in uniform and out of it, who believed a few years ago that their lives were their own, walk towards the Horse Guards, show their passes, and branch off — each to his own prison-house, where he will spend the day in activities for which he knows that his life was not designed. Moving among them are American soldiers on leave who tug at an English heart by asking the way to Buckingham Palace or where they should go to set their watches by Big Ben. We, who are familiar with these local marvels, turn aside, go with the American, ask him of his own ; and how eagerly he will tell of them — of the great lakes, it may be, or the tobacco country, or the glittering winter on the border of New Hampshire and Vermont — always with the question in his mind of how the world will be changed when he goes home at last, the question of values, of what is constant and what variable ! Nothing so actively prompts this questioning as the visible persistence of peaceful detail among the general condition of war. Hardy comes back :

7

Reflections in a Mirror

> Yonder a maid and her wight
>   Come whispering by :
> War's annals will cloud into night
>   Ere their story die.

And to-day a man and a girl, miraculously at leisure, seated under a tree in St. James's Park, or indeed the ducks and pelicans themselves, the constant pelicans whom none can conscribe, create not simply the romantic nostalgia that the future-gazers contemn, but a mental friction such as produced Hardy's verse in another time of " the breaking of nations ". The friction arises from a rubbing together of the superficial habit of mind into which, as exiles from our true lives, we fall continually, and our deeper, almost buried apprehensions of the truth. An artist, condemned to be an official, sees through the prison walls of his officialdom ; a farmer, now a soldier, remembers the origins of his life and puts his soldiering into a tolerable pair of brackets ; a girl, harnessed in a uniform which she had been in danger of supposing to be a part of herself, sees even this abnormality in the perspective of her youth. So it happens that, instead of resigning themselves to their lot or rebelling against it, they make a genuine acceptance of it — that is to say, cause it to become for them transparent or, better, translucent ; and, rejecting the lie that " nothing will ever be the same again ; the old world is gone ", answer : " I am not gone and I carry my world within me ". They evaluate themselves, each asking the questions that bear upon his or her own nature and discovering in the debate a light here and there on the movement of civilization itself. "What is worth dying for?" is seen in its relationship with "What is worth living for — and in what order ? " — a question as hard and personal now as at any time in history. To ask it continually, and to ask it with reason and compassion, is the purpose of the imaginary debates in which these essays have their part.

On Being
Born Now

WHAT will he be who is twenty-five in the year 1968
— the child born now? There is none who will not
hope that he may enjoy a better world than this; and there
are few, alas, who will not tell us, in terms of their social
prejudice, in what the improvement is to consist. One
says that the young man is to have " a higher standard
of life ", another " a classless society ", a third " freedom
from war ". He is to have a more elaborate complex
of wants and the means of satisfying them; he is to
receive more pay and work less for it; he is to have
two bathrooms, a wireless set, an aeroplane, equality of
opportunity and a refrigerator. He is to have, he is to
have — yes, but what is he to be? — believing what?
valuing what? It is not an unpractical question. Men
and women, except the scum, live and die for what they
are, not for what they possess or may acquire. Except
a few gangsters and tradesmen, no one will gain by this
war; nevertheless, it is being fought to the death, an
economic futility which is not, and is not felt to be, futile.
Is the world mad? The tradesmen say so. Nevertheless,
it is, as a fact, the world. Men and women are living
and dying not for gain, and, except the scum, not for
comfort or security. And yet what is, seemingly, being
planned for the young man of 1968 is a more and more
richly endowed materialism on an equalitarian basis. Is
this what he will desire? Is the man who would desire
this, or be satisfied with this, the creature whom we
imagine and whom our imagining will create?

To say what we desire him to be is as hard, and hard

for the same reasons as the writing of autobiography. There is no difficulty in saying what we wish him to have ; the more we claim for him the more generous we shall appear to be and the more be applauded ; but to predicate his essence, the manner of man he shall be, the values precious to him, is to confess ourselves at least by implication, and that needs the courage which Rousseau had even unto the little shames, or Montaigne's love of men combined with his indifference to their opinion of him. For reasons that are evident from Murmansk to Minnesota, it is, for example, perilous to say that we hope for, and expect in, this young man a power to reject the vice of mass-thinking. And it is equally perilous — because it invites attack by all those in whom resistance to sentiment has become a gross sentimentality — to confess a belief that if he writes, he will value Turgenev ; if he draws, Ingres ; if he loves, Héloïse ; if he plays music, Chopin, for his passion as well as for his form ; and if he thinks, Dante. He may, without affectation of conscience, permit to himself and to all men the possibility of privilege and elegance as a part of endeavour's legitimate reward ; he may reject, as principles and as attainable practice, all equalities except equality before God and before the law ; he may value order more highly than we, because he values freedom more truly ; but he will not think of order, in the totalitarian manner, as an escape from individual responsibility. Rather will he value it the more for being the product of self-discipline, an intuitive function of " l'âme bien née ", and the less for being — what it must nevertheless remain in certain departments of life — a function of the State. In brief, he may have included and absorbed our separated freedoms in the one freedom to which our organization of collective opinion has been for a long term of years increasingly opposed — the freedom to think, and may regard it as being his first duty to himself and society to exercise this freedom. To suggest this in a world where a group-mentality still controls many of the instruments of power is the more dangerous because the control is slipping. Nothing is more provocative to men whose claim to attention is that they lead the vanguard than to show that their fashion is spent, that the young are in full revolt against them, and that the child born now may grow up to despise them. But there are good reasons for believing this to be true.

The men whose teaching is being repudiated, the stale vanguard of the twenties and the thirties of this century, urged upon their generation the belief that a man should not think of himself as an individual but as a member of a group, a class, a party. To this belief and the surrenders included in it they gave the general name "social consciousness", and so brought into their fold many innocents who thought that by this phrase was meant the loving of one's neighbour. Social consciousness, in their own different and narrow sense, the stale vanguard applied to their interpretation of all life and all art. Whoever did not profess it was outcast. They ignored Moore's funeral; they spat upon the poetry of A. E. Housman within a few days of his death; they applauded T. S. Eliot while he made his individual pilgrimage through a waste land which they considered their own, but became less enthusiastic when he refused to be their dutiful tenant and emerged into a positive faith independent of class and party. For it was the essence of their rule that any external allegiance of the individual was a betrayal of the group; to love God or love England was to deplete the energies which might otherwise have been wholly devoted to the pursuit of heretics. Moreover, to love God or to love England or to practise art in any name but that of social consciousness was to generalize, and the most honest of their self-deceptions was a belief that intellectual or emotional generalization was necessarily false — except in the domain of politics where the supposedly "exact" science of economics redeemed it. Lest it should be supposed that they are being misinterpreted, let Mrs. Woolf speak of them. She spoke with sympathy, but to the same effect :

So then our contemporaries afflict us because they have ceased to believe. The most sincere of them will only tell us what it is that happens to himself. They cannot make a world, because they are not free of other human beings. They cannot tell stories because they do not believe that stories are true. They cannot generalize.

That is to say, they were in a state of helpless self-contradiction. Each could tell us only of his subjective experience considered in isolation from the experience of humanity, and yet each clung to his group, his coterie, and was incapable of any generalization extending beyond it. Mrs. Woolf wrote this fifteen or more years before the outbreak of war in 1939, and she wrote it of "them" in their relationship to literature. It was equally true of them in their attitude towards life, and, as the years passed, it became increasingly true, so that they were utterly blinded and frustrate — before war came, denying its approach, refusing to prepare for it ; when it had come, embarrassed to discover that the foreign enemies of their group were also the enemies of their country ; and at last, when Russia was attacked, seeing in this German stroke a miraculous escape from their confusion. Ever since, they have preened themselves upon that vast military organization beyond the Niemen as though it were the answer to an advertisement in their parish magazine.

Such were the men of the vanguard. The final condemnation of them as men of imagination is Mrs. Woolf's : "They cannot tell stories because they do not believe that stories are true ". They could not tell stories or " make a world " because they were timid of vision, because they did not dare to imagine. Life was to them a tessellated pavement on which they stepped delicately from stone to stone, holding one another's hands, partly for comfort in the touch, chiefly to be sure that no one of them should rashly take wing. The only muse they would allow was the spiteful, which they dignified with the name of the ironic. When Eliot praised Kipling, they revolved miserably in their communal grave. Their voice to-day is that of a shrill ghost whining its indignant protest against those who have advanced beyond it, but they still command certain instruments of critical opinion and political comment, and as soon as there is peace these dead will rise again. They will tell the young that only Philistines love their country. They will repeat that stories are not true, that to generalize is to be a false romantic, that no tale is worth writing without a snigger and no life worth living until it has become a disillusionment. They will say that truth consists in the note-book of a " mass-observer " and in repudiation of such pretty simpletons as Keats. Much depends, indeed almost everything (including the peace of the world) depends, upon whether the young man who is being born now accepts or rejects these intellectual justifications of despair. The power of these men depended upon the skill with which they played upon the emotion of self-pity, and self-pity may be created. First, you promise to your partisans a new heaven and a new earth at no cost to themselves ; next, you lie in wait until it is evident that the promise cannot be fulfilled ; finally, while proclaiming an anti-romantic doctrine in all else, you romanticize the consequent waste-land. The safeguard against this propaganda of disenchantment is a preliminary realism — a refusal to believe that universal suffering is a title to personal reward. To this degree of realism, which is identical with the so-called romanticism

13

of Turgenev, those who fight in this war seem to be approaching. The young man of 1968 may have attained to it.

We hope — but how little, at this range, we may presume to understand him ! Underlying the superficial motives of conquest and revenge with which the German leader has inspired his nation, there exists, not as the occasion of this war but as the cause of the series of wars in which we are engaged, a desire, shared by all peoples, to re-define the concepts of freedom and order. This desire expresses itself in a hundred ways — in the ignorance and prejudice as well as in the aspiring wisdom of mankind — and has long been stirring. Nearly half a century ago it turned England from mere jingoism to a complete reimagining of Empire ; to-day, in those parts of America which are unaware of that act of reimagination, it is throwing up a demand for a change already in great measure accomplished. In Germany and in Italy it has assumed what we consider perverted forms : and the history of the Russian revolution itself may be regarded, by opponents as well as by adherents, as the history of a struggle to give expression to it. Everywhere, and with varying consequences, there has been evident this desire to re-define freedom and order and to re-state the relationship between them. The name given to this struggle, when at last a name is given, may well prove to be a heading to the chapter of our times in the history of the world.

By 1968, the confusion of ideas inevitable during the early decades of the defining process may have ended, and a man aged twenty-five have begun to see his way. Two things above all others are to be desired for him : a confidence in his own individualism and an assurance that by being true to himself and accepting responsibility for his own attitude towards life he can best serve the community. In the essay which has already been quoted,

Mrs. Woolf, writing in the twenties, pointed out that, in literary criticism, there was no one corresponding to Dryden or Johnson or Coleridge or Arnold. Not that any one of these great men was " an impeccable judge of contemporary work ". Their mistakes were notorious. " But the mere fact of their existence had a centralizing influence " — an influence that Mrs. Woolf found to be wanting among her contemporaries. The reason she gave was that a great critic can arise only in a society ripe for him, and society was not ripe. " Our age is meagre to the verge of destitution. . . . It is an age of fragments. . . . Much of what is best in contemporary work has the appearance of being noted under pressure, taken down in a bleak shorthand which preserves with astonishing brilliance the movements and expressions of the figures as they pass across the screen. But the flash is soon over, and there remains with us a profound dissatisfaction." Was not this true of the life as well as of the literature of the time ? Did not the weakness arise from deliberate refusal to choose, to maintain, to accept responsibility for a point of view ? No Dryden or Johnson or Arnold could exert " a centralizing influence " because the whole tendency of the age was centrifugal — a throwing out of sparks, not a concentration of heat and light. It was for this reason a deeply unhappy age, so bitterly aware of its inadequacy that it sought wild compensations, organizing itself into groups or surrendering to the "leader-principle", as a lost and panic-stricken child will hide its face in the skirt of any passer-by, only to look up presently into the eyes of a forbidding stranger.

This compulsion of fear may have been lifted from mankind when a child born now approaches his maturity. If so, the effect upon literature must almost certainly be an effect of integration. What will be the nature of this integration none can foretell, but that literature will cease to be, in Mrs. Woolf's sense, fragmentary is scarcely to be doubted. Variety may well be increased rather than diminished ; it is fear that produces uniformity — there was a dreadful, protective likeness among the fragments of the twenties and thirties ; and the Renaissance was as various as it was bold. What may be coming is a determination to see, and having seen to express, things as they are — neither resting content to record external appearances nor twisting interpretation into conformity with a programme. Revulsion from the late languors of Romanticism has produced in our time an opposite extreme, a harnessing of thought, an acceptance of blinkers vilely called " ideological ". These having been cast off, young writers twenty-five years hence may be choosing subjects and employing forms that we do not dream of. What matters is that they shall find their subjects within themselves and that what they write shall be, not notes "under pressure, taken down in a bleak shorthand ", but a distillation of personal experience not felt to be personal only — in brief, that they shall be unafraid to generalize or to believe that stories are true.

To be unafraid and yet to be free implies an assurance that order is not opposed to freedom or even external to it but is an element of it — a thing without which freedom itself is not and cannot be. It is towards this concept that mankind appears to be struggling. The British Commonwealth is an evident attempt to give political expression to it beyond the boundaries of a single nation. Future attempts in the same kind but on an even larger scale and adapted to the needs of peoples not subject to the Crown will depend, in the long run, on the power of individual men to realize this concept in themselves — on their power to create freedom within the self-discipline of " l'âme bien née ". How is the child born now to win this power ? It must come to him, if it comes at all, through his renunciation of the things opposed to it

— of the doctrine, for example, that order is the product of a collective tyranny and a personal surrender. This doctrine, from the extreme Left to the extreme Right, has convulsed the twentieth century. It is blessedly improbable that the child born now will grow up with a taste for it. And is there not hope also that, once liberated from it and impelled by nothing more obscure than the old Adam in him, he may grow up into that glorious and amusing being, a Character, which we, for a hundred reasons of social conformity, have done our utmost to suppress? He will scarcely be such a Character as Landor was; the centuries do not repeat themselves; but it does seem not unreasonable to hope that the twentieth century may, before it is done, so powerfully revolt against mass-thought that Characters (now called freaks) may re-emerge, and ordered freedom rediscover herself in their responsible and undaunted individualism.

The Integrity of Pascal

THE first of the many delights that spring from Dr. H. F. Stewart's edition of " Pascal's Apology for Religion " * is the thought that at this time it should have been published at all and that the editor should have been enabled to hold in his hands this reward of long devotion and scholarship ; the second is the reminder it gives that Pascal's work continually transcends its immediate purpose and is of value to men and women of our own day who may be little inclined to express their problems in terms of the Christian faith. The confusion of the papers that Pascal left behind him at his death has been the opportunity of learned men for two hundred and eighty years. He had intended to distil from his wisdom an ordered and conclusive *apologia* for his faith. Thoughts and arguments had been written down, but their ordering was unsettled when he died and can never be settled now. Nevertheless he was said to have delivered a lecture, probably in 1658, in which he described to his friends the plan of the book he had in mind. An account of this lecture is given in the " Discours sur les pensées ", attributed to Filleau de la Chaise, and in the preface to the " Pensées " by Étienne Périer, Pascal's nephew. The " Discours " was designed as an introduction to the 1670 edition of Pascal's remains. It was rejected by Pascal's sister, Madame Périer, in favour of the preface by her son. Dr. Stewart, in an appendix, prints both texts and compares them in parallel columns. They and his own knowledge — and, even

* " Pascal's Apology for Religion ", extracted from the " Pensées " by H. F. Stewart, D.D.

more valuably, that love of an author which endows research with a saving intuition — have guided him in his attempt to select and arrange the unsystematized *pensées* as Pascal might have wished them to be arranged within the framework of the book he contemplated. The result will no doubt be a subject for debate among Pascalisants — a highly technical debate of exclusion and inclusion, of placing or misplacing, from which those of us who are not specialists will do well to abstain ; but, as we come in from our walk across St. James's Park, we may be glad to discover at the fireside a volume so coherent, so evocative of the heart as well as of the intellect of France, and so close to our hopes and fears.

"My object in this volume", says Dr. Stewart, " is to present in a reasonably coherent form material which, even in its broken state and despite the obvious desuetude of some of its arguments, is a very present help for all who seek to champion the Christian Faith." It is more than that. Those whose intellectual direction is away from Christian dogma or who, at any rate, have become accustomed to approach the problems of their own belief from an untheological angle may still find that Pascal is a present help to them ; for, though his argument is for his faith, his method is, in the noblest and freest sense, humane ; he is an artist who happens to be applying his art to theological uses, and the language of whose thought is so far from being conventionally pietistic that modern men and women, who are of sceptical mind but not of irreligious temper, find to their surprise that it is their own.

This is the wonder and greatness of Pascal, the origin of his power to be renewed in each succeeding generation. Except the callous and the defensively frivolous, there can scarcely be a mind that will not discover companionship in his — companionship, moreover, of the sort that is to be had only of the intimate giants in whose thought we discover continually, or seem to discover, a projection of our own, in whose lucidities we recognize, as it were, a cipher to our own confusions. A scientific mind has satisfaction in the lovely blending in Pascal of accuracy with imaginative sweep. One may disagree with him, but the nature of the disagreement and the point of divergence are always clear ; he does not hedge or fluff. A philosophic mind has corresponding rewards, for, if Pascal's premises be granted, his logic is cumulative and natural, converging from many angles upon the truth. An artist, too, finds in Pascal a mirror of his own purposes — a desire for beauty not as a vain decoration but as a means of truth ; and men who are not artists or philosophers or mathematicians, who would speak of themselves, perhaps, as " average men ", well knowing in their hearts that they inhabit a solitude of self, find that Pascal has the privilege of entry into their solitudes and of speaking to them in their own most secret language. Some who are aware of his reliance on the doctrine of the Fall or of the importance he attaches to Old Testament prophecy may be inclined to echo Dr. Stewart in speaking of the " obvious desuetude " of some of his arguments, and may suppose, as Dr. Stewart certainly does not, that he has nothing to give them which they can hope to accept ; but no one can read Pascal without coming to understand before long that what is important in him, apart from his doctrinal conclusions, is his insistence upon the value and necessity of a quest for truth. His address is always to men who have lost themselves, who feel that they are drifting aimlessly down the little stretch of river between birth and death, who are unhappy because they can see no design in their lives, and who have tried, without success, to blind themselves with passions or to lull themselves with a protective indifference. To them he says, in effect, that the little stretch of river is incomprehensible apart from its origin and its end. He personally is assured that Christianity supplies a complete chart and is determined that his reader shall be led, through faith and reason, to the same conclusion ; but before attempting to prove his case — " avant que d'entrer dans les preuves de la religion chrétienne " — he insists upon the folly of men's indifference to the quest of truth, " une chose qui leur est si importante et qui les touche de si près ", and the argument which follows is one that presses even harder upon us than upon his own contemporaries. He speaks of the man who is not only indifferent but is proud of his indifference. He confesses that he has no words in which to describe " une si extravagante créature " ; then, in a magnificent passage, allows the extravagant creature to speak for himself.

This is Pascal's method from first to last. He is not an aloof lecturer but a dramatist of the soul. As a novelist puts into each of his characters, into Vronsky as well as into Levin, a part of himself, so Pascal allows those who are the protagonists of his argument to speak out of his own experience, to re-express the doubts that he has overcome, to advance the sceptical reasoning that his faith has transcended, to be revealed in the confusions from which he himself has emerged. To prove this from his biography is impossible ; too little is known of his early life ; one cannot say with assurance : " Here and here Pascal is referring to this or that aspect of his personal struggle ". But there is evidence of that struggle not only in the text of the " Pensées " but in the nature of their impact upon ourselves. Other men, writing from the point of view of a faith firmly established in themselves, are apt to alienate their readers by using the tones of a too comfortable authority. Having, as they believe, arrived, they forget the journey, the weariness and the doubt, the falling by the wayside which is, perhaps, their readers' present experience ; and their readers put away the book, saying : " This man cannot help me ; he seems not to have come my way ". Pascal, on the contrary, gives the impression of there having been very few ways that he has not tried. He has the compassion that springs only from having suffered. He seldom condemns, preferring always to pity, and reserving his invective to be used against those who make a vanity of indifference.

Again and again little phrases look out from his text, not with the forbidding stare of final authority, but with the eyes of the pilgrim that he was — and still is as he writes. These phrases, implicitly autobiographical, are never spectacular and may easily be overlooked. For example : he says that there are three kinds of men — those who serve God, having found him ; those who, not having found him, " s'emploient à le chercher " ; and those who live without seeking him. The first are reasonable and happy, the last are " fous et malheureux ". Then he adds the revealing phrase : " Ceux du milieu sont malheureux et raisonnables ". Does anyone doubt that he is speaking from experience ? " Malheureux et raisonnable " has the ring of memory in it. And it is always in such phrases as this, which are personal to him, that he bridges the years and speaks to generations not his own. Are there two words that more closely describe modern men of good will than " malheureux et raisonnables " ?

It would be foolish to insist overmuch on this autobiographical or confessional aspect of the " Pensées ". Anyone who will may reply that what we feel to be autobiographical was nothing of the kind and that, when Pascal allowed a free-thinker or an indifferentist to speak aloud, he was doing no more than dramatize his argument as Plato dramatized his in a Socratic dialogue. Very well ; but this much at least is sure — that Pascal was prevented by something within him from treating the opponents of his argument as mere ninepins, put up insecurely that they might the better be knocked down. He was never so eloquent as when he spoke for them or — may it be said ? — when they spoke for him. There are passages more stately, more agile in reason, more richly jewelled than these, but there are not any that have the same directness, the same tang. When this free-thinker of the seventeenth century speaks, one seems to hear at one's side the voice of a young man of the twentieth, and yet, looking into his face, to discover the eyes of Pascal :

En voyant l'aveuglement et la misère de l'homme, en regardant tout l'univers muet, et l'homme sans lumière, abandonné à lui-même, et comme égaré dans ce recoin de l'univers, sans savoir qui l'y a mis, ce qu'il y est venu faire, ce qu'il deviendra en mourant, incapable de toute connaissance, j'entre en effroi comme un homme qu'on aurait porté endormi dans une île déserte et effroyable, et qui s'éveillerait sans connaître où il est, et sans moyen d'en sortir.

To be carried in sleep to a desert island, to awake in fear, to wonder, to ask, to have no answer — has not this been for years the theme of contemporary verse ? Has not the desperate and agonized desire for any answer rather than none lain at the root of the perverted materialism of the totalitarian creeds ? Freedom becomes insupportable to a man when it makes him feel that he is " abandonné à lui-même ". If he is without breeding or tradition he springs to the conclusion that all values are dissolved about him, declares himself " incapable de toute connaissance ", and flings himself at the feet of a Leader, as a frightened and ageing woman may fling herself into a dishonourable marriage, not, as her friends suppose, for material gain, but in an attempt to annihilate her identity.

What Pascal thinks of as indifferentism has, then, precisely what we should not expect it to have — a link

in motive with totalitarianism : the link being a refusal to ask questions, a desire to suspend criticism, an
incapacity to supplement reason with faith, and faith
with reason, a slave's willingness to separate them, a
fanatic's longing to keep them apart. This particular
complex of motive, this black despair of which the negative expression is indifferentism and the positive totalitarianism, is the sin that Pascal does not forgive. He
will not allow the island to be made barren by a divorce
of the values which, in conjunction, make it fruitful and
an origin of the great voyages of the spirit. Always Pascal
is " raisonnable ", but his reason instructs him that
Reason is not truly reasonable which will not recognize
its own interdependence with means of wisdom external
to it. Ralph Hodgson has the spirit of the " Pensées ".

> Reason has moons, but moons not hers,
> Lie mirror'd on her sea,
> Confounding her astronomers,
> But, O ! delighting me,

has an origin in Pascal himself :

Le cœur a ses raisons que la raison ne connaît point : on
le sait en mille choses. . . . Nous connaissons la vérité, non
seulement par la raison, mais encore par le cœur ; c'est de
cette dernière sorte que nous connaissons les premiers prin-
cipes. . . .

In this firmness, there is reassurance of a kind that is
to be found in few professed apologists for any faith.
Pascal's faith is never isolated from its intellectual context
or from the promptings of the heart. It is neither sentimental nor cold. Fanaticism, like fear, arises from a
split in the human personality ; faith, and Pascal's con-
spicuously, from an integration of it.

It is for this reason that his work " transcends its
immediate purpose ". Even those who reject some or

all of the dogma that he accepted find, underlying his particular arguments, a general thesis that now engrosses the whole world. What is the division among the peoples? Is it not a division between those whose hope of mastery depends upon a disintegration of the human personality and those whose political and moral systems depend upon the integration of it? Some will have it that the war we fight, not in the field only but in our minds and hearts, is for " democracy ", others that it is for " freedom ", others that it is a vindication of the Christian way of life or, at any rate, a struggle against forces which, if they triumphed, would make even an approximation to that way of life impossible. Through these and many other differences of interpretation runs always a deep reluctance among discerning and unhysterical minds to attribute a fundamental evil to our enemies. There seems to be an arrogance in making such a charge. Who are we to judge? we ask ourselves. What right have we to restate a political dispute in terms of moral absolutes? A phrase from a verse written in the last war — " God this, God that, and God the other thing " — satirically warns us against appointing the Deity to the Chiefs of Staff's Committee. Are we not English? Is not compromise a virtue? It is a political virtue, but it can be a moral vice — the same vice of indifference, of avoiding responsibility for spiritual decision, that Pascal condemned. Is it not true that what we are opposed to in totalitarianism is a polity possessed of the Devil? Is there not implied in it a will to overthrow the balance of judgment, to disintegrate the spirit of man? We may answer yes or no, but we cannot shrug our shoulders. Pascal compels us to decide.

The Return
of France

MANY years hence, when the events now in the future * have fallen into the perspective of history, three friends, French, American, English, seated together at a table — perhaps at a little table on the Quai d'Orléans — may watch Notre Dame rise against the night sky of early summer and say : "A June night, and no war !" And say : "Then civilization had its opportunity, its last chance". Across the years, we, who shall have been long dead, may now hear the following pause but not the reply that will break it. Was the chance taken or missed ? What will then be the place of France in the world ? In what mood will the Englishman and the American have visited Paris — in that of an alien "bourgeoisie" gaping at the relics of the past, or in that of men who have learned and understood and been permeated by the civilization of France ? And the Frenchman — how will he think of his guests and how consider the months which began in the early morning of November the Eighth ?

Among English, French and Americans there are differences of temperament which, in many instances, are irreconcilable. No purpose is served by denying them, and none by extending to include the French who, least of all, are to be deceived, those blurred courtesies with which Americans and English too often seek to obscure the plain outline of their prejudices. In 1940, the French surrendered. What is harder to endure, they appear to have believed, as Germany and many Americans did, that we also should surrender. Afterwards at Vichy

* This essay was first published on November 28th, 1942, three weeks after the landing in Africa.

men in power declared, in terms not attributable to duress, their desire for a Germany victory, and elsewhere — even in the freedom of America —there were Frenchmen who gave with their pens a positive support to the enemies of France. What can be forgiven in a tradesman and perhaps forgotten in a politician is unforgivable in an artist, as it is in a priest. Their vocations impose upon them an absolute honesty. Others may compromise, they may not. Among Frenchmen, unquestionably artists, there were some whose hands shook. None of this is a reason to condemn France. If we were to begin to count the sins and failures of her children and to match them with our own, or weigh against them the opposite heroisms and loyalties that Frenchmen have to their credit, we should be lost in unending debate and fail to discern what the problem really is with which the modern history of France has confronted the world.

A nation, in its influence upon civilization, is not an aggregate of its living people, for they are but a part of the whole continuing and historic people. Nor is it a State, for the State is artificial. It is an Idea. As behind the features, the diverse characteristics, the conflicting acts and appearances of a man, there is an individuality which is himself, so behind a nation there is an idea, and, proceeding from all nations, a confluence of ideas into the stream of civilization. There are other ideas, not national — the Christian idea, for example, or the idea of scientific inquiry — which flow into the main stream partly through the national tributaries, but also independently of them. The importance of the national ideas remains. If we fail to distinguish the idea of France among the confusions of the contemporary scene, we shall be in danger of committing a sin against ourselves and against civilization.

There is a quality or art, for which no recognized

name exists, that is to statesmanship what statesmanship is to politics — that is to say, it underlies statesmanship, its material is not humanity to-day or humanity to-morrow but humanity itself ; its responsibility is not to the decades but to the centuries. Call it for convenience the art of primary statesmanship. A primary statesman's aim is to prevent the stream of civilization from being poisoned, to preserve its energy and fullness, to use it for the irrigation of those areas of experience which are or may become barren, to defend it against those whose policy is to dissipate or disintegrate it. He sees past, present and future not as a sequence but, with a painter's eye for his canvas, as a single composition. A Secretary of State for Foreign Affairs may be a primary statesman also. As Secretary of State, he is concerned with nations, with the interaction of their manifest powers, and to this is bound by his special duty ; but as primary states-man he is concerned with the ideas of nations : the two points of view are as different — and as interdependent — as those of policeman and priest, of journalist and historian, of chronicler and poet. From one point of view he regards behaviour, appearances ; from the other, essences. With one voice he asks what the French have done, are doing, will do ; with the other, what France has been, is, and is becoming, what Germany has been, is, and is becoming, and so the pressure of events is lifted from him, the noise of party is quieted in his mind, fore-sight and memory become vision, he has courage in judgment, sureness in love. If ever he has loved France, he is able to see her as now she appears to be and yet pay to her, to her essence, the supreme tribute of Ras-kolnikov, as he knelt before Sonia : " It is not to you I kneel but to suffering humanity in your person ".

The idea of a nation changes. The identity remains, as the identity of a human being remains through all the metamorphoses of character ; John grows older, he hardens or softens — becomes, we say, " a different man ", yet he is always John ; his innocence is in his guilt, his hope in his failure, his childhood in his age. In that sense, the sense of identity, France is always France. But the Idea of a nation is mutable, it may be corrupted so that it poisons the stream or be enriched and purified ; and the error into which we English may fall is to believe, because Frenchmen have betrayed her, that the Idea of France is corrupted, and to believe, on the contrary, because there is lazy and complacent vanity in the belief, that the Idea of Germany is not corrupted. If we make these mistakes or either of them, if we open the dams to the German stream before it has been purified by the passing of many years or close them against the French, it were better for us not to hear the answer of our descendants as they sit together on the Quai d'Orléans.

What is the Idea of France ? Behind her action and her thought we may discern, as in the " Pensées " of Pascal, the idea of integration. The French have an abiding tendency to think in terms of the individual— then, jumping all intermediate steps, in terms of France. This tendency is evident in their approach to the art of government. They have so strong a natural reluctance to think of themselves in groups, so great a distaste for working, as we say, " in a team ", that a party-system as stable as ours or the Americans' is scarcely conceivable among them. The peculiarity of their constitution, which denied to a defeated President of the Council the right to demand a general election, was a proximate cause of the insecurity of their governments and of the fragmentary divisions of their Chamber, but the reason for these things lay deep in a Frenchman's unwillingness to delegate to a group any part of his intellectual independence. The French Revolution itself was stamped with this reluctance. Its revolutionary forces were further from unanimity than revolutionary forces have ever been ; dog ate dog with astonishing speed and regularity. Even when the tide was in flood, criticism, which in Germany hides its head at the first challenge of power, survived stubbornly, for France requires a corrective to every enthusiasm, for every Bonaparte a Talleyrand, in every revolution an inheritance from Voltaire. It is for this reason that she is so often an irritant to Anglo-Saxon enthusiasts who are in haste for a new heaven and a new earth, and it is true that she has the defects of her quality. But let us first of all recognize, even in the field of politics, her quality for what it is — not negativism, not obstructionism, not mere cynicism, but a profound historical sense of the fallibility of groups, a feeling that collective enthusiasms detract from individual integrity, and a desire, for the sake of that integrity, to dissect every enthusiasm and to insist always, as fanatics do not, on the interdependence of faith and reason.

Englishmen often object that the French are too drily logical, that they are without faith, incapable of vision, hard. Before examining this view, let us again admit the defects of the French quality and, in the defects, see the quality implied. Are they " hard " ? Yes, in many things — in criticism, for example. They have none of our tendency to let down lightly the failing powers of a one-time favourite of the theatre ; but remark this — they will not attack an actress because she is old and far older than her part, but they will not spare her, old or young, if her performance itself has deteriorated. This is contrary to our sentiment. We are by tradition gentle with the corpses of the theatre if once they were beautiful. In this the French are harder — but are they not truer ? In the theatre, in literature, in politics, they have none of our charitable loyalties to past glories when the actual performance weakens. Their criticism is directed to the performance itself. If it is good, no extraneous circumstance will cause them to discount it ; if it is bad, they will admit no plea in mitigation of its offence. So when a great singer's voice begins to fail, Paris is no place for him ; so, after Sedan, Bonapartism vanished like a puff of smoke ; so, amid all the present uncertainties of France, we may be certain of one thing — that the Third Republic is dead.

The charge that, in her quest of " realism ", France fails in vision is a more serious one. It is said, for example, that in her insistence on formal pacts and her suspicion of all looser ties between peoples she failed, during the last quarter of a century, to give their true value to the imponderables of politics. The same charge — and it is worth remarking that it is spiritually the same charge — is made against the French language and litera-ture. It is said with truth that the French language, though capable of great magnificence and of extra-ordinary lightness, though brilliantly precise, accurate and unambiguous, is yet limited by the difficulty with which its words can be persuaded, even by poets, to carry meanings other than those assigned to them by the dic-tionary — in short, to accept overtones. It is said, further — and again with truth if we insist upon discussing French literature in terms of our own — that the great outpouring of genius which French writers have given to the world is disproportionately weak in the quality of mysticism — not only, shall we say, in the quality of Vaughan or of Blake, but in the " imponderable " vision of Coleridge. This charge may be debated on its own ground, but it is better to shift the ground a little and, leaving for the moment unchallenged the religious mysti-cism of Vaughan and Blake, to reply with the mystical absolutism, called symbolism, of Mallarmé and his heirs for here is the French genius expressing itself in its own way — seeking always greenness within green things, the essence within appearances, the single within the many, the integrity that shall include and reconcile the dis-

integrated — that shall ultimately (if Mallarmé had succeeded) annihilate the disintegration of experience. His
path and Blake's do not intersect ; but they are parallel,
and it need not surprise us, when we ourselves attain so
far, to discover that they meet in infinity.

Whatever aspect of French life is submitted to analysis,
the ruling passion to avoid dispersal, waste, irrelevance,
to see things as they are and to bring them into their
true relationship with one another, to create a reasoned
whole out of seemingly diverse and irrational parts, in
brief to integrate, is everywhere apparent. France's will
to do this has long been her value to Western civilization
and the reason for her having been for so long the uni-
versity of the world to which painters, writers, philosophers, men of science, and youth itself have come, not
so much for the instruction she could give as because
she was, they felt, a mirror in which they might have a
new reading of themselves. She had her faults. In
recent years they were intensified. No one who knew
her well could be unaware that she was frightened and
that fear had made her fiercely and at the same time
uncertainly defensive. The idea of France, the idea of
integration, was being threatened within and from without by enemy fanaticisms. She was tired. After the
recovery of the seventies, after the struggle and bleeding
of the second German war, she was passing through one
of those periods of her immortality in which she felt herself to be very old, and her enemy was preparing to
strike again. He struck and conquered. His method
after conquest was what it had been in preparation for
conquest — what the method of totalitarianism always
is : to disintegrate the human personality by offering to
weary and impressionable men the opportunity to col-
laborate in a false, artificial and tyrannical unity.

In fact, totalitarianism precisely corresponds in the life
of nations to insanity or possession in the life of men.

It consists in the destruction of all values but one — the value of power ; the annihilation of all private virtues but one — the virtue of obedience ; the poisoning of all reason and all faith that may act as a corrective to a single fanatical exaltation. The consequent overthrow of the balance of the human mind and of its ability, dependent on the preservation of that balance, to criticize experience and to distinguish between good and evil is a wrong far greater than all the physical abominations of the Nazi method, a wrong equivalent to the corruption of the soul. Yet there are still good men and good women who believe that what we are now fighting and France is suffering is no more than the ambition of a gang, and who .count it for virtue and moderation in themselves to deny that we are at grips with a spiritual evil that has possessed a nation. Yet the truth is being written in France for all to read. In Poland, which has never been, like France, a centre of European integration and is regarded by Germany as a material impediment to expansion eastward, the policy of extermination has been enough, but in France, because France is trustee of the central idea of European civilization, the policy has not been to exterminate but to divide, humiliate, corrupt and use. If by force of arms we drive the enemy out, the policy, though in a different form, will persist. What Germany is fighting for is not material conquest only but conquest by spiritual disintegration. To this are opposed the idea of Christianity, the idea of compassionate justice within a rule of law which lies at the root of the English-speaking democracies, and the idea of integration embodied in France. For that reason she is necessary to us and, if she can be corrupted, necessary to Germany. Our attitude towards her will become increasingly a test of our wisdom. Whatever nation — America, England or Germany — looks into the face of France may, if it will, read its destiny there.

The Idea
of Europe

UNLESS we are uncommonly arrogant or insensitive, it may be a shock to all of us, Americans and English, to discover, in the time of liberation, how deeply ignorant of Europe we have become. Awareness of the Danube and the Vistula has never been among the besetting virtues of the Five Towns or of the Middle West, but in the past at any rate we have been able to send out scouts, to receive visitors, to import books. Now for years our European communications have been for the most part official or clandestine. Sometimes a book circulated by the French resistance movement reaches England ; sometimes a Frenchman or a Czech or a Yugoslav comes out of the darkness, bringing us tales of what he has seen by the light of his little torch ; but how slight our knowledge is, and how far we are from being able to compose such fragments as we have into a recognizable portrait of Europe ! It is as if pieces of a human being were described to us — the curl of the upper lip or the movement of an eyelid — and we were to attempt to build with these pieces an appearance, an individuality. It is impossible. If the pieces were a thousand times more numerous than they are, it would still be impossible. What we lack is the living presence, the *feel* of Europe.

Nevertheless we try, and are bound to try, to make provision for her future. Responsibility for her life will fall heavily upon us. The devil of it is that we are in the position of a doctor called upon to prescribe for a patient he has not seen or of a young man asked to fall in love by correspondence. Being Americans and English, ever given to good works, we shall not shirk the task,

but again, being Americans and English, ever inclined
to see others in our own image, we are in great danger
of lavishing our care, curative, educational or sentimental, on the wrong lady — or, indeed, upon a lady
who does not exist at all. If anything on earth is certain,
it is that Europe is not thinking in our idiom or desiring
what we would have her desire. She may, indeed, be
envious of some of our freedoms, but it by no means
follows that she wishes to play the game of politics or
of life in our own or in the American way. She may,
for example, entertain the ideal of self-government in
one of its many forms without in the least desiring to
imitate the working of the American Constitution or of
the Mother of Parliaments. In brief, what are benefits
to us may be to her impracticable and even ridiculous.
What is elixir to us, she may vomit. While we are writing
our prescriptions it is as well that we should understand
who the patient is, and how proud she is, how deeply
rooted in her own history, how different from ourselves.
It may even be salutary to recognize that, as we hurry
into the sick-room of Europe with our stethoscopes
and our remedies, the patient will often say (or think) :
" How kind of the barbarians to send their doctors to
me ! "

Goethe said to Eckermann in 1825 that all Englishmen
were incapable of reflection ; they could not find leisure
to cultivate their minds, but were great in practical affairs.
This opinion is part of Europe's inheritance. It is directed
now towards Americans also ; and we shall do well to recognize the fact, for, if ever there was a man with title to
the name of European, Goethe was that man. It may,
of course, be answered that no one is entitled to that
name, and that Europe is no more than a geographical
expression. And yet Europe is a condition of thought.
In Russia the controversy about Turgenev largely turned

upon whether he had or had not become " europeanized ", and the idea of Europe as an entity, a distinct influence upon thought and manners, reaches far back into Russian history. The English and the Americans, though they may always have been hard put to it to give a positive definition of Europe, define her by implication when they recognize her difference from themselves and from the Eastern and Middle Eastern peoples. The ideas of the Roman Empire, of the Papacy, and more distantly of Athens, have all served to establish, as a reality in the human mind, the idea of European coherence. If it were not a concept with power over thought, the Germans would not have troubled to represent their aggression as an attempt to establish a new European order. Nor would they have obtained as much credence as they have received. Quislingism and collaboration are not a product of cowardice alone or of selfishness alone. If they were, there would be no distinction between Pétain and Laval. Often collaboration has had its origin in a subtle perversion of the European idea — in the belief, held by many faint-hearts in 1940, that as one of the English-speaking peoples had been driven back to its own shores and the other showed no signs of issuing forth, European civilization must somehow save itself, even by accepting German leadership.

In this matter, as in so much else, the Germans have been, up to a point, exceedingly astute, and have brought their astuteness to nothing by a fundamental egoism. Recognizing what we are always in danger of failing to recognize — the existence and power of the European idea, they used it, against us and against Russia, as the basis of their appeal. Europe, they said in effect, is in need of a new integration. Europe must cohere in a new order and discover a new centre of gravity, In this, they were echoing Goethe, two of whose sayings are very much to the point. To Eckermann Goethe said :

I have no fears whatever for the French, they have reached such a height in the history of the world that their genius cannot possibly be suppressed.

And to Kozmian :

The-French nation is a nation of extremes, it knows no moderation. Possessing as it does tremendous strength, moral and physical, it might lift the world on its shoulders, could it but find the centre of gravity. But it does not seem to know that he who would lift a great weight must find its centre.

The modern Germans have never ceased to be uneasily aware of the truth of the first saying. Paris has had for them an irresistible fascination. They have approached the civilization of France as a jumped-up and ambitious tradesman approaches an artist or aristocrat — now flattering it, now striving to humiliate or corrupt it, and proving always their sense of its inherent superiority. And they have applied Goethe's second saying, not to France, but to their own Weltanschauung. Assuming that it is necessary for some power to " lift the world on its shoulders ", they have so misread Goethe as to believe that when he said " tremendous strength, moral and physical " he meant, or ought to have meant, " ideological and military " ; and they have vitiated their appeal to Europe by insisting that in Berlin and only in Berlin shall its centre of gravity be found. Their understanding that such a thing as Europeanism exists is to their credit and might have been their contribution to the history of the twentieth century ; but it is the fate of the Germans that their materialism always curdles their mysticism, their philosophy is corrupted in action by their terror of being despised. They have therefore perverted their own truth, have imposed their egoism upon it, and are a warning to us not to repeat their error in terms of our own power or even of our own idealism.

The temptation will present itself in the subtlest of

all forms — the form of necessity. When this war is done, there will lie before us a disorganized Europe. Every bandit and self-seeker will rush in for loot. Every fanatic of evil and fanatic of good will wish to apply the hammer of his own fanaticism while the iron is soft. The task of leadership in western Europe will impose itself upon us, particularly upon the English, and though it is extremely unlikely that a desire for military domination will lead us to pervert the idea of Europe, for temptation does not present itself to the English or to the Americans in that form, we can by no means be certain, if we examine ourselves, that we may not unwittingly repeat the fable of the Fox and the Stork — inviting our guest to a banquet of all the virtues but presenting them upon an Anglo-American dish to which she is by nature unaccustomed and from which she cannot eat.

Among the hardest of our self-disciplinary tasks will be that of restraining ourselves from mentally arranging Europeans in our own categories of virtue and vice. What we consider a " backward " citizen is not necessarily a bad citizen in many parts of Europe. If we offer to the peasants of Montenegro a political system or educational institutions which seem good to us, we may be offering them what is, in their eyes, contemptible or even immoral. In that case, those who hurry into our fold may, by the standards of their own people, be degenerate renegades, and we should be on our guard against the schoolmaster's error of assuming that the docile are the virtuous. Let us beware of those who come with comfortable assurances that they desire nothing so much as that their children be nourished on the pure milk of English compromise and receive afterwards the unspeakable benefits of an American education. The great men of Europe and, if you will, the good men are those who dream their own dreams, not ours, and as their dreams differ from ours so also do the direction of their faith and the nature of their integrity.

Nor is this true of Montenegrin peasants alone. It is equally true of highly cultivated men in France, Austria, Italy, who, because they have knowledge of our way of life, may the more easily lead us into the error of supposing that they differ, or ought to differ, very little from ourselves. Europeans have great difficulty in understanding that, under the strange reticence and uniformity of manner that the English have imposed upon themselves in the last hundred years, there still exists an attainable warmth and variety of character. We have a corresponding difficulty in understanding that, in Europe, variety of character survives near the surface of behaviour, and that a European is not necessarily unreliable because his manner is, by our standards, " eccentric " or " affected ". Americans are less likely than ourselves to make this particular mistake. They have not our rigidity of manner ; but they are even more easily shocked by those whose social or moral conventions differ from their own. They find it hard to look upon a rose without wishing to reform it. For these differing reasons both we and they are in great danger of misjudging a cultivated European — we of believing that he is dishonest because his argument is dramatic and his behaviour extravagant ; Americans of thinking that he is, in some obscure sense, faithless to civilization because he is sceptical of transatlantic enthusiasms.

If a sense of that danger is always present in our minds, we may approach our task with at least a reasonable hope of surmounting the first obstacles. An attempt to put Europe to school, however benevolent the education proposed, is doomed to failure, for Europe is beyond school-age. In part mature, in part savage, she is like some beautiful and cultivated woman in whom an ancestral wildness survives, and to treat her as if she were naughty and ignorant is to be ridiculous. It is useless to protest that she has made a mess of her own life by living it in her way and should now try to live it in ours. Unless we should decide to isolate ourselves from her — which we English at any rate could not do if we would — our only course is to learn to speak European and, in order that we may learn, first of all to recognize that there is such a language. " C'est une langue nouvelle qu'il faudra bien que l'on apprenne ", said Briand in the context of Locarno. We may adapt his saying and acknowledge that European is an extremely ancient language which it is necessary for us to learn, for though it is true that at Locarno the Powers made, or appeared to make, a new attempt to speak an international language of European peace, it is true also, in a different sense, that there has always been an idiom of thought, a way of life, which, however unprecisely, may yet with general truth be called European. That it is uniform no one pretends ; every attempt to give cultural or religious or political unity to Europe has failed ; but the attempts, the very failures, are proofs of the stubborn and recognizable existence of a European idea and that one of its essential qualities is variety. Even though we are wise enough not to arrange Europeans in our moral categories, and discreet enough not to imagine that they will look for their salvation on any blackboard of ours, we may yet, if we do not beware, commit the damnable error of treating the house of Europe, which is old and rambling and various, as if it were or ought to be a gigantic string of factories awaiting the glorious improvement of being " rationalized " by us.

Those Englishmen and Americans upon whom European responsibility falls will be beset by pressure from among their own people, urging that there is here an opportunity, not to be missed, of calling into existence this, that or the other Utopia. Their answer, if they are to avoid the confusions of partisanship, must surely be that they exercise a dual function : first, as victors in a great war, they are to safeguard the peaceful interest of their own peoples, depriving potential aggressors of the means of aggression ; and secondly, they are trustees for the recovery of European civilization and not dictators to Europe of her way of life. To reconcile these two duties, to preserve a judicial distinction between them, will require an extraordinary exercise of imaginative statesmanship and a rare steadiness of purpose. In democracies the steady application of judicial principle to foreign policy is exceedingly hard, and may, amid the confusion of domestic politics on both sides of the Atlantic, prove to be impossible after this war, unless the Press and the people are themselves willing to exercise an uncommon patience. They are unlikely to do so unless statesman-ship treats them with exceptional confidence, and speaks " explosive thoughts " fearlessly, as General Smuts has done.

To say " this high matter of Europe is above the heads of the people " and make no genuine attempt to explain it to them is, in the present condition of the world, to court disaster. Democratic statesmen make a profound mistake when they " play down " to their electorate. European policy is, indeed, a " high matter " ; the less reason for obscuring it with such catchwords as " peace in our time ", and the more reason for patiently expound-ing it. The task before Anglo-American-Russian states-manship is not to write to-morrow's headlines or a hasty pamphlet flattering to partisans, but to make possible the slow composition of a masterpiece — a new volume in the History of Europe. It can no more be written than any other masterpiece if the work is continually interrupted, and its design continually broken down, by ignorant clamour for results. It will be said that poli-ticians cannot afford to be " academic ", and that they are now addressing themselves to so vast a concourse that they are bound to " play down ". To say that is to leave the democratic system to founder. Democracy cannot continue in the world unless it distinguishes between long-term statesmanship and short-term politics, and it will be a test of our power to make this distinction that we recognize the idea of Europe as a thing not rooted in our particular idealisms.

A Leisured Civilization

THE day may not be far distant in which it will be a principal anxiety of statesmen, economists, educationists and of all others that have charge over us to persuade mankind to take holidays — prolonged, magnificent, undreamed-of holidays. Why? All that we can tell is that the wise men are hinting at it. Their argument seems to be roughly this : that the engines of production, built up for the purposes of war, are now so gigantic that, when the demands of war and the immediate demands of reconstruction cease, there will be a glut — which they call over-production — unless measures are taken to prevent it. Therefore more men must take more holidays and go about the stern business of uninterruptedly consuming. There is much more than this to the wise men's argument — the balancing of goods and money, for example — with which we groundlings do well not to entangle our ignorance. What emerges for us from their discourse is the discovery that they are now seriously addressing their minds to the problem — disastrously neglected since the industrial revolution began — of how to persuade machines to yield, and men to accept, a dividend or wage expressed in terms of leisure. They are attempting to give an answer to those who have long declared that machines have been an uncivilizing force because, instead of releasing man from labour, they have in fact added to his enslavement. To put it with crude simplicity : there were the machines, ready to do a great part of our drudgery for us and let us go out to sing and play, to enjoy our lives and refine and decorate them, or, if it amused us, to become philosophers. But we multiplied our wants and our numbers to provide more and more work for the machines ; we magnified our wars in order to glorify them ; and we ourselves herded into cities and clocked in to serve the machines. Now at last, say the wise men, we have reached, or shall soon reach, a limit to all that. Their argument leads to the conclusion that before long they are going to send us out into the fields to play or become at any rate — so far as the machines allow — part-time philosophers.

The idea is not altogether new. The seventh day and even that enlightened institution which, in America, is called the Sabbatical Year were invented some time ago. In Paris of the eighteenth century, before the blessings of the Revolution were shed upon it, the idea was prevalent among master and man. " It was Sunday : and when La Fleur came in, in the morning, with my coffee and roll and butter, he had got himself up so gallantly arrayed I hardly knew him." All this finery, readers of. " A Sentimental Journey " will remember, because La Fleur proposed to beg the day off " pour faire le galant vis-à-vis de sa maîtresse ", a request with which it was extremely inconvenient for his master (who proposed the same occupation for himself) to comply. But Sterne was a tolerant and civilized man. He recognized virtue in the French rule of holiday-making :

Happy people ! that, once a week at least, are sure to lay down all your cares together, and dance and sing, and sport away the weights of grievance, which bow down the spirit of other nations to the earth.

The new idea of the wise men is not new, but it will prove to be none the worse for that, so long as it have the effect of letting civilization out of the industrial cage.

But who has not, in his time, courteously and with exalted motive, opened the door to a caged canary and been disappointed ? The poor bird grows accustomed to his perch ; even the nursery table becomes for him an alarming wilderness ; put him out upon it, take your eye from him, and in a moment he is hopping back again to his bird-seed and water. Even a canary becomes an economic bird in the end, and the wise men, having for so long trained mankind to believe that bird-seed and circuses and chromium-plated swings are the highest rewards of civilization, and that they are available only to faithful inhabitants of the industrial cage, may find that civilized man, when put out on the nursery table, is filled with sudden panic and is by no means prepared to sport away the weights of his long grievance. In that case, the educationists will have to take their turn. They will have to retrain the reluctant bird to endure the responsibilities of freedom — and, since the ways of educationists are slow, the reluctant bird will have to do something to retrain himself. In brief : if men are to have more leisure, they had better learn what to do with it.

There are two good uses of leisure : the first is to pursue an activity that pleases you — in which may be included anything from a study of Plato to La Fleur's sabbath occupation ; the second is to be idle. Idleness has long had its defenders ; it is a pretty subject for essayists ; but most of them, in writing of it, have confused it with the other use of leisure — the pursuit of a pleasant activity — and have explained how they occupy their idleness on their favourite pastime, fishing, reading, a game of patience or what you will. But idleness ought not to be occupied at all. It is of its essence that it should not be. It should not be occupied even by designed and consecutive thought. Thought, it is true, refuses to cease, but it can be persuaded to drift ; one can haul down its sails, release its helm, and listen to nothing but the small inconsequent chatter of the stream of consciousness, " What a waste of time ! " the improvers cry. " Have you no better way than that of spending the precious hours ? " " None," the good idler answers, " there is none better — and, if it is profit you are looking for, none, in my experience, better rewarded." Idleness, unbetrayed by consecutive pastimes — pure idleness, that is to say — is like those magical instants between sleeping and waking, at night and in the morning, when the burden of intellect is lifted, and the spirit, no longer stifled by doubt and struggle, breathes freely, and goes out upon uncharted voyages and, swift as Ariel, brings undreamed-of treasure back.

Will not the educationists themselves consider this and take it into account ? Will not priests ? They are concerned not with the mind of man only, nor with his mind and body only, but with the spirit of man. It is madness, and a way to madness, to allow children no chance to be idle. How many schools there are, or were, whose whole life is work or games or sleep or entertainment ! If the boy is not at the blackboard, he is on the football-field ; if he is not playing, he is on the touch-line cheering others while they play ; if he is neither working nor playing, he is being herded to a lecture, a concert, a play — even a movie ; or he is asleep. Idle hands, it is piously believed, will always find their way into Satanic mischief — an ignorant and indeed an impious belief, the truth being that idleness is an opportunity of the spirit, an opening of windows to its outgoing and incoming, and that whoever, in his arrogance, tries to bar out Satan by the shutting of that window, slams it not in Satan's face only. There are too many in authority over the young who believe either that there are no angels or none but the fallen. They may be easily recognized. Ask them, if they keep school : " What opportunity will my son have for idleness ? " and they will think you mad if they can be persuaded to believe that you are serious.

They, too, often without knowing it, are keepers of the industrial cage. Idleness is not, as these taskmasters

46

suppose, a barren unemployment of the mind, but one of the arts of life. It is a means of dissolving the clouds with which experience darkens originality. Who has forgotten the idle hours of his childhood before the routine of school engulfed him ? — hours without clock or purpose, eternities of morning between breakfast and midday, in which life was not a measured acre but a receding horizon of associations. The grasses then were forests or an assembly of spears, the spears grew suddenly and went marching through continents, and there, at the lawn's edge, was the sea, which parted so that the people went over on dry land ; who, when they had crossed over, were changed, dissolved, forgotten, other timeless images taking their place, a silence falling where the rhythm of their feet had been, and voices shining in the silence. For, in those hours, a voice might shine and a shaft of light have music in it, as they may even now between sleeping and waking ; the senses were merged in a single awareness ; consciousness was transferable — you were the earth you trod on and the air you breathed ; you were the younger child you had been and the man you would become ; yesterday, to-day and to-morrow lifted you upon an indivisible tide and, when the mountains sang together, it was in the course of nature that they should.

Since then the many glories that are one have been split into their intellectual divisions. The early gods are fallen ; Thea mourns at Saturn's feet. The usurpers of man's natural kingdom have regimented him to work and games, and have forbidden him his creative idleness. "What opportunity will my son have to be idle?" is a question to be asked not only of schoolmasters. It addresses itself to all the wise men who are planning our business in the coming world.

Nevertheless, there is another use of leisure by which

the activists may be better pleased — the doing of things that are delightful and are not felt to be drudgery. Even this is hard for modern men, though not so hard as true idleness. It is hard because the same taskmasters who have cast upon idleness the shadow of vice have put pleasure under suspicion or at any rate poisoned it with the idea of utility. What gives deceptive strength to their argument is that usefulness can, in fact, so often be pleasant ; all work is by no means drudgery ; but it does not follow from this that leisure ought to be useful or that we should frown upon those in whom it is not. If, as the wise men hint, we shall before long be threatened by the danger of over-production and if, this time, the remedy for it is not to be the artificial creation of new wants in an ever more laborious community, but the establishment of a new leisure, it will clearly become a civic virtue in a man to abstain from using his hours of ease in earnest productivity. This applies as well to an artist as to a collier or a clerk. A writer or a painter, though he love his work and his tools lie ready to his hand, must have the courage of his leisure — the courage, that is, when he has laid down his pen or his brush and has said : "Here my holiday begins !" to take his holiday and to find pleasure in other things than his art.

It is a hard saying. Always at his back an artist hears Time's wingèd chariot ; he aches to be at work again ; but the ache is that of a smoker for tobacco withheld from him — an ache which, in the end, diminishes and gives the mind peace. "But I do not want the ache to diminish !" the artist exclaims. "I want to be at my canvas again ! What other pleasure is there ?" This is what we have to learn — that even though our work is delightful there are other delights, and that it will be necessary, in a newly leisured civilization, to cultivate them. Leisure is, or should be, a corrective to extreme specialization, enabling men to know them-

selves and enrich their individualities. It is an occasion
for shoemakers to abandon their lasts, and for schoolmasters to lie fallow, to forget that their profession is to
correct, and to meditate upon those defects in themselves
and in mankind that are happily incorrigible. It is for
all of us a liberating meditation, a humane means of
self-healing and self-knowledge, corresponding to the pre-
scription — now, alas, rare among doctors — of a glass
of port. Self-knowledge comes from many sources : from
suffering, in which our generation is well schooled ; from
labour, from concentration, from the quest of perfection ;
but it comes also from variety and spaciousness and
delight.

In these things, our generation is greatly impoverished.
It does not think so, or did not, until lately, begin to
think so. The Victorian age was full of voices proclaiming new marvels and those who cried that man was being
drained of his individuality cried then in a wilderness.
We, too, have been guilty of a corresponding delusion —
not, in the Victorian manner, a complacent one, not
morally comfortable, but nevertheless a delusion of
intellectual richness — a belief that, because we had
explored every corner of our cage and pecked at every
bar of it and knew the difference between bird-seed and
sugar, we were masters of the known world. And yet
how much of variety we had never known that Cellini
knew ! What an extraordinary impression of spaciousness
one receives from reading the lives of even little-privileged
men of the eighteenth century ! Poor hacks, we say,
how hard they worked and how little they were paid !
How slow and uncomfortable were their journeys, how
defective was their sanitation, how low their standard of
living ! And yet how little rushed they seem to have
been. If their journeys were slow and uncomfortable,
they were shorter and fewer than ours. How much time
they had for letter-writing and conversation and the

quiet reaches of friendship ! They seem to have had the gift, whenever it suited them, of sitting down at the roadside in the shade of a tree, or, better still, of withdrawing with Amaryllis into a meadow, and of letting the wingèd chariot go hurrying past. This capacity, this variety, this gift of leisure, the machines have taken away from man, and shall now — so the wise men say — restore to him.

For such a recovery we shall have to pay a little in pride and prejudice, but we dare not refuse the price. A leisured civilization, knowing how to use its leisure, is, and always has been, the true and natural product of a machine age. What must come is a vast distribution of leisure at the expense of the machines. The question is whether those who might have it will now willingly accept it. Leisure, once lost, is hard to recover. It cannot be snatched at. A man who, having worked without a break for two years, finds himself suddenly with a few clear days can do little with them. He cannot " unwind ". The old tension holds him. Leisure is a habit of mind, and only in long untroubled holidays can the habit be recovered. An enlightened cooperation will be needed to make this possible : an almost revolutionary boldness in employers ; a willingness among employees to see their new holidays not as a chance of hasty, crowded entertainment but as a new spaciousness affecting the whole range and speed of their lives ; and, above all, among educationists an eagerness to show men what they are and not only what they may do or earn. Nature is at our service, her power infinite and available. Soon the door of the cage will be opened. Shall we accept freedom, or are we so tame and greedy that we wish for nothing more than a new lump of sugar thrust at us through the bars ?

Why
Birds Sing

HOW the mind travels in these days of war ! Except to those on warlike missions all England's gates are locked, and the names of foreign places acquire for the rest of us the power of an incantation. Enclosure gives new sharpness to our old envy of migrating birds, and for compensation we return to the books of Hudson and Selous and Delamain — a wise and peaceful inheritance. Some, it may be, in their desire for foreign places, are systematic even in their obsessions, and allow the hand that takes down a book and opens it to be guided by their interest in current events.* They go with Horace to call upon that officious innkeeper — " Tendimus hinc recta Beneventûm " — or learn their strategy with Hodgkin, remarking the importance of the town to the Lombards, " blocking the great high-road between Rome and Constantinople, and cutting off the Romans on the Adriatic from the Romans on the Tyrrhene Sea ". That no doubt is the profitable way in which to transcend the pains of geographical claustrophobia, and those who are capable of it will learn much, but we are not all capable of it, our dreams outrun the armies, and suddenly we are in the Duomo at Lucca before that wonderful tomb of Ilaria whereon she, a girl, lies sleeping,

her gentle face calm with included vision, her eyes but lately closed. Over her limbs and feet, at which a dog is resting, her drapery lies in austere folds. Her hands are simply crossed, not at her breast or in any symbol, but as they might have been when she slept . . .

* Written in October 1943, when the army of the Allies was near Benevento.

and below her, on the sarcophagus, are Jacopo della Quercia's naked, curly-headed boys, festooned with fruit and flowers. How little strange it is, how natural with a naturalness transcending all the accidents of history, that she should be sleeping there while the English light falls on this page and, in Italy, the English armies look northward ! Why is it that though time and division blur the memory of friends so that by their absence they are, in a measure, lost, there are, for each one of us, works of art invincible against oblivion ? Friends, when found again, are changed. They marry and are given in marriage. But Ilaria and her garlanded boys will not change, even though the marble be broken, but will be bathed always by " a serene light within the idea of melancholy " which was the Renaissance, and which, since the Renaissance, the world has lost.

To such journeys, grave or gay, the mind requires but the lightest incentive. The pelicans of St. James's Park, long familiar to the passer-by, one morning set a half-remembered tune running in his head and are straightway the occasion of an Egyptian flight :

> We live on the Nile. The Nile we love.
> By night we sleep on the cliffs above.
> By day we fish, and at eve we stand
> On long bare islands of yellow sand.
> And when the sun sinks slowly down
> And the great rock walls grow dark and brown. . . .
> Wing to wing we dance around,
> Stamping our feet with a flumpy sound ;

but the virtue of the pelicans is not that they lead to Egypt but that, when their daughter came out, they gave a party which all the birds attended.

> Thousands of Birds in wondrous flight !
> They ate and drank and danced all night—

and to think of birds is to think of Jacques Delamain,

and to think of him is to think of France and his country
of the Charente, and it is in France, not Egypt, that we
would be. The great rock walls that grow dark and
brown

> Where the purple river rolls fast and dim
> And the ivory Ibis starlike skim,

are no doubt of romantic appeal to many an exotic taste.
Pelicans and ibis are unquestionably someone's enchanted
birds, but it is permissible to find a deeper enchantment
in watching, with Jacques Delamain, the circuit of the
titmice and their companions.

Birds have — or seem now to have — something in
common with the figure of Ilaria, sleeping in the cathedral
of Lucca. They are, like works of art, exempt from
human taint, and, however fierce in themselves (and the
titmice are by no means gentle), have not our collective
and enslaved ferocities. They do not spend their lives
in doing collectively what they hate doing and are not
constrained to do by any natural pressure. Unlike men,
they do not contradict their own reason, thwart their
own instinct, or organize their own destruction, with
proud insanity, in an attempt to obtain what they cannot
define and do not need. It is, therefore, dangerously
easy to be sentimental about birds and to value them
"picturesquely", as if their existences were without peril,
cruelty or unhappiness, and there is nothing to be gained
by falsifying them. But there is, equally, much to be
lost in refusing to be comforted by their detachment from
human life. Consider the dreadful alternative. Man is
an interfering creature. Who doubts that, if he had been
capable of it, he would have tamed the birds in order to
instruct them in his morals and confer upon them the
benefits of his civilization? As it is, he has been able
to do no more than cage or shoot them, which is at any
rate better than humanizing them. But his incorrigible

tendency to make all other creatures dependent on himself might conceivably not have failed, and birds, instead of being, as they are, separated from him, might have become his pets, his sycophants, even his pupils. Thereupon he would have begun to criticize and, in accordance with his own lights, to improve them ; he would have tried to educate them and might even have succeeded. Whoever had said, at this stage of the procedure, that it would be better to let the birds go, for their natural state was wiser than their reformed condition, would have been told that the defects of that condition were but transitional, that more time was needed, that the birds were humanized not too much but too little, and that, in denying this, he was a pessimist and a reactionary.

Fortunately birds have made unnecessary a philosophical battle for their independence. A few have weakly consented to eat out of man's hand ; a few more, the least intelligent of the species, have been domesticated by him, and so have lost the power of flight ; certain parrots have deigned to mock him ; but the rest, being highly intelligent, wary and observant, have decided that for them the good life is that which has least contact with men. As it is comforting to know that, though we may destroy a work of art, we cannot debase the art which was its essence (Ilaria being thus exempt from our folly though marble is subject to guns), so it is pleasant to reflect that, in birds, there is a life which all our knowledge is powerless to corrupt.

It is not an emotional exaggeration, but simply true, to say that birds have upon man an influence of purification and redemption. In his darkest hours, when it seems to him that his own kind has spread a blight over the whole world, they are for him a visible reassurance to the contrary. We have been told by the Tharauds, Jérome and Jean (who, in their introductory letter to

Why Birds Sing

" Why Birds Sing ", use the first person singular, as if the two of them were one), how, in the war of Fourteen, they went bird-watching with Jacques Delamain in the trenches :

From August, 1914, until May, 1917, we shared the fortunes of the same regiment. In Flanders, in Soissonais, in Champagne, during the monotony of those interminable hours — so short to-day in the remoteness of time — I see you again leading me, your head bare contrary to all orders, like the real rustic that you are, carrying, slung over your shoulder, the field-glasses that never left you, not for the purpose of watching out for Boches, but to go looking for the bird of the season in the spring foliage or on the dry branch of winter. You would tell me like a tale his adventurous history. He was always arriving from some unexpected country, from Greenland or Equatorial Africa, from America or India, that little bundle of feathers you were pointing out to me. . . . Throughout your narratives all those winged lives, so full of miracles, would carry away the imagination into lands bordering on the realms of fable and mythology. We would make our escape there all the more willingly because this swift and free race was really the one which, at that moment, we would have wished most to resemble.

The translators are right. " Celui auquel, à cette minute, on eût souhaité le plus ressembler " — to " resemble " is the word ; but might not the Tharauds have written, with a deeper truth, " to be " ? . . . Certainly the men who watch birds, having begun by discovering in the life of " ce peuple libre et rapide " a reassurance concerning life itself, undergo a certain metamorphosis. They do not begin to resemble birds physically, as a groom or a hard-riding lady may begin to resemble a horse. How should they ? — for the appearances of birds greatly differ and an ornithologist would be hard put to it to reconcile in himself the outward livery of a marsh-titmouse, la jolie Mésange Nonnette, with the silky splendours of the great crested grebe.

No : he does not, because he cannot, become birdlike, but he does, metaphysically, become bird, in the sense that, while remaining human and lovably human, he engenders within himself a blessed detachment, a grace of penetration, an exemption from our grey sorrows. He uses his vision, like the birds themselves, " non pour guetter les Boches ", and in his writing there is for us that quality of redemption and reassurance which has been spoken of as residing in birds themselves. It cannot be for the sake of the Charente only — there are, perhaps, lovelier rivers — that the mind now returns so ardently to Delamain's countryside, and yet there are moments when it seems that peace and sanity will not have come again until he is seen bareheaded, with field-glasses slung about him, coming out of his miraculous wood. " October ", he wrote in prelude to his titmice —

October has already tinted the tops of the poplars with yellow, plated the dark green foliage of the elms, in spots, with gold, stippled with russet, here and there, the oaks on the border of the wood. The mingled bands of Titmice begin to form.

That was written more than fifteen years ago, and to-day it is a matter of faith to believe that, in the same quiet spirit, he is watching, as they assemble, " les acrobates du monde ailé, les exploratrices infatigables de chaque branchette ", and that some day we may watch them with him. And in the evening ? " After a battle and before a marriage — always a glass of cognac." It will be the time and the place.

Meanwhile there are his books. Let us recall them. " Pourquoi les oiseaux chantent " and " Les Jours et les nuits des oiseaux " have appeared in English as " Why Birds Sing " and " The Days and Nights of Birds ". " Portraits d'oiseaux " was published in Paris in 1938. In the spring of 1939 " Les Oiseaux s'installent . . . et

s'en vont " was still an unfinished manuscript ; it will
have been completed, perhaps, before now. " Why Birds
Sing " was crowned by the Academy. In England it
and its successor were greatly praised and widely read.
Delamain was not denied his rank, and yet, though all
who have read " Why Birds Sing " treasure it, and
though to be a lover of it is almost to find oneself a
member of a recognizing brotherhood, there are people
who have never heard of it. Now, there are many who
have not read White's " Selborne ", but there is none
that has not heard of it or does not intend to read it
to-morrow, and " Why Birds Sing " has always stopped
short of fame in that degree, the fame of complete acceptance which is, precisely, the fame it deserves ; for it is
not a specialist's book, not a manual for ornithologists,
but a universal work of art so simple in structure, so
unselfconscious in manner, that the unwary, enchanted
by its warmth and grace, might be tempted into saying
that it was not a " work of art " at all but the talk of an
angel invited to the nuptials of the little owls and the
woodpeckers.

It must, however, be admitted that Jacques Delamain
is not, in any hierarchical sense, an angel, though they
who are would not find him conspicuous in their company.
The first part of the truth is that all Frenchmen know
how to use their language and he knows better than most,
and the second part that he writes with love of a subject
that is — and the phrase is used deliberately and with
its full meaning — his second nature. He does not
" resemble " birds, but he knows what it is to be bird,
and so adds to his power of human observation a veritable
compassion, a faculty of loving from the inside outwards.
When he tells, in his essay called " Les Noces ", how the
birds re-dress themselves for the spring, there is no
doubt that he himself, in his second nature, has known
what it is to put on a stonechat's new coat :

The vital pressure of the first fine days brings about a slow modification in the aspect of a bird. At the end of summer, stripped, by the moult, of his plumage, faded by sun and rain and worn out by the labour imposed by the rearing of the young, he had dressed himself in the more sober livery of winter days. Now, the colours brighten up. The falling of the fine ends of the feathers reveals, bit by bit, the fresh hues they covered, washes breasts with bright green, coppery red and poppy colour, and adorns mantles with every shade of grey and brown. Or else, only certain parts of the plumage are touched by the invisible artist, who lays a spot of deep black on the breast of the Grey Wagtail where pale yellow used to prevail, hoods with dark brown the head of the Black-headed Gull, caps that Yellowhammer with a golden helmet, shades with carmine the breast of the Linnet, freshens a superciliary arch, and augments the tones of a dress, matching or contrasting. Often the metamorphosis seems sudden, and it is astonishing to see, on a day in February, the dull Chaffinch of winter months and the little sooty Stone-chat, who flutters over the bushes, appear in their fresh wedding suits with shining white that comes out on the dark background of their coats.

It is not a purple passage, for the book contains none, and at first a reader, who comes upon it thus in isolation from its text, may say : " Yes, it is well done ; it is accurate observation of the life of birds ; it is valuable to ornithologists ". But let him hold the book in his hands. Let him read on about the friendships and hatreds of birds, about the spring and autumn migrations, about the great pauses of February and August in the rhythm of nature, and he will find that it is of creation that he reads, of life in the midst of death, of light in darkness. There is a Magnificat in this book and a Nunc dimittis and much that, being understood, passes understanding. It is, like Ilaria del Carretto and like all those rare works of art that have the divine quality of being beautiful without being proud, a mirror in which man, considering himself in a great darkness of the soul, may see at once his peril and his salvation.

Under the branch weighted down with snow, along the rugged trunk, is a tuft of feathers, an inanimate thing which one might think was last summer's nest. The hand drawing near to grasp it is surprised by a warm contact. It is a cluster of Goldcrests, eight or ten chilly little bodies, who have pressed close to one another, placing their hope of salvation—

but let Delamain speak in his own tongue—

" plaçant leur salut dans la somme de chaleur que leurs duvets réunis peuvent opposer au vent glacé ". On these frosty days one sometimes finds on the ground in the forest, among the faded leaves and moss, dull as these and undiscernible were it not for the tuft of glowing flame, the body of a Goldcrest, dead of cold.

It is plain enough ; there is no symbolism in it ; and yet it is a way out of prison. It is a Frenchman who offers it. A means of approach to the English is often to be found through birds and animals. Would that " Why Birds Sing " were in the hands of them all ! There is no acceptable currency between nations that distrust one another except genius and goodness, the gold and the silver. All else is propaganda, the devil's dross, which will buy none but fools.

The Heritage
of Symbolism

READERS are naturally suspicious of criticism's attempts to classify artists ; so, indeed, are artists themselves. What does it matter by what name we call such a man as Baudelaire ? To Saintsbury he appeared as a second flowering of Romanticism. Dr. Starkie, in her new edition of " Les Fleurs du mal ", has recalled that it was once a habit to speak of him as a Parnassian — for no better reason, as it now seems, than that some of his verses found a place in that extremely public omnibus " Le Parnasse Contemporain ". Dr. Bowra treats him as a Symbolist, together with Mallarmé and Verlaine. Is all this no more than pedantry ? So sweeping were the genius and influence of Baudelaire that there were letters for him in all the pigeon-holes of inspiration, and those he sent out have since found their way to every address. Man is unique. Is not analytical criticism, of which classification is a part, necessarily a waste of time ?

Sometimes it is. Chatter of " schools ", of " movements ", of what in America are called " trends ", is dangerous if it tempts the critic to swerve from his true art of individual interpretation and leads him to overstress resemblances or differences which happen to suit his theme. Nevertheless, an artist, however individualistic he himself may be, cannot be " read " in isolation ; he is a part of the book of his times. To speak of Romantics or Parnassians or Symbolists may lead to a folly of label-hanging but is more often an honest and necessary attempt to see artists in their relationship to one another and so, in the long run, to life itself. For the very reason that each man is unique and that this is the central fact and miracle of creation and the denial of it the central blasphemy, a connexion between the supreme individualists — that is to say, between poets — is, where it can be truly perceived, of transcendent interest ; "transcendent" because, wherever that connexion is something more than an artificial alliance between members of a sect, it exists, not upon a level of common interest or common ambition, but upon a transcendental plane and is an indicator of truth. The artificial grouping of poets into "schools" for no other reason than that they may thus be made to fall easily into the chapters of text-books is a vice of pedagogues, but to discern the common spiritual origin of men so diverse as Baudelaire and Stefan George or Mallarmé and Alexander Blok is much more than a virtue of scholarship ; it is, in the world's present condition, a service to mankind.

This service the Warden of Wadham, in his account of Valéry, Rilke, George, Blok and Yeats,* and of their connexion with the symbolism of Baudelaire, Verlaine and Mallarmé, has performed in a way that gives excuse for believing that he himself is modestly unaware of the breadth and depth of his book's appeal.

Some years ago I wrote, for my own satisfaction, and with no real intention to publish, a series of essays on some poets whose work meant much to me. I have at times showed them to friends, who have pressed me to make a book. They tell me that there is a general interest in these poets and that some account of them is needed. . . . This book makes no claim to learning or scholarship or to be anything more than an attempt at explanation and criticism. . . .

So be it. The implication is that those who already have some knowledge of Valéry and Alexander Blok may be glad to have their knowledge extended, and certainly,

---

* "The Heritage of Symbolism", by C. M. Bowra.

for them, these essays are indispensable ; but they have another importance which the author does not claim. There are many thousands, to whom Blok and Stefan George are scarcely names, who might find in this book a map to unexplored territories in their own minds. It has, in the first place, the merit of lucid exposition ; it describes the poets of whom it treats, and describes them comprehensively, with sympathy and justice, never seeking to manipulate them as the puppets of a theory, never with patronage of the poor, ignorant reader who does not happen to be the inmate of a sect, caring always and only to discern the poet's intention and to interpret the poetry accordingly. In this respect the book is an open window upon the stuffiness of much contemporary criticism, which has a habit of examining the masters' work as politicians examine their rivals' speeches — for what in them can be perverted or used. Dr. Bowra is just, even in his quotations — and he provides translations of the German and the Russian. The passages he gives are so abundant and representative that an initiate in any of his subjects is able to make fair test of his argument and a newcomer may feel that he is being honestly led. But this is by no means all. It is possible to be thus a genuine interpreter of particular poets and yet to write a book of little value except to professed students of poetry ; but sometimes criticism, without diverging from its subject, extends its range, so that a reader, from a better understanding of particular poets, is drawn on to a better understanding of poetry itself, and of the age in which it was written. The period which Dr. Bowra discusses is the half-century intervening between 1890 and our own day. It ends with Yeats. If we ask why we are what we are and, even, what we are becoming, we may find here the poetic aspect of the answer or, at any rate, the material with which to build an answer for ourselves. These poets are not interesting for technical reasons only. They are, if

Dr. Bowra has rightly chosen them, what Baudelaire called " Les Phares ".

The book is, then, to be considered as a whole, for its flavour, the direction of its thought, above all for its special relevance to the study of contemporary values. Its peculiar merit invites so broad a treatment, for though it is detailed and highly specialized where detail is illuminating, the post-symbolists are not seen in isolation but in a long perspective. A novel or a play, if it has genuine quality, does not begin at the first page or end at the last, but leads on the imagination to ask : " What was ? " and " What will be ? " Books of criticism, on the contrary, have a habit of stopping dead. Their subject seems to be enclosed by the rim of a microscopic slide. When it has been intensively studied you feel that nothing remains to do but to put it away in a cupboard and turn your attention to something else. But Dr. Bowra's essays are so written that the continuous connexion, the interweaving, of art with life is apparent in them. They are, in brief, not narrowly technical discourses but humane meditations.

As criticism, the most brilliant is the opening discussion of Paul Valéry. Valéry is the outstanding modern instance of the fusing, in poetry, of the intellectual and the emotional impulses, and so, in success and failure, his work is a scale by which modern poets may measure their own. His direct influence in England has probably not been great, for the plain reason that our knowledge of his language is seldom of the deeply familiar kind which enables a reader to be so perfectly at ease that he can " let nimself go ", can yield himself to the overtones of words. The problem is complicated by the fact that though Valéry, being French, very rarely permits himself obscurity of language, and, sentence by sentence, has a clarity that flatters the understanding, he yet, in " La Jeune Parque ", could write what, with good reason, " has been acclaimed as the most obscure poem in French ". It is impossible to give a plain and single answer to the reader who asks : " What is it about ? "

" La Jeune Parque ", Dr. Bowra says, " has been variously interpreted as the monologue of a Young Fate who has to choose between celestial seclusion and earthly responsibilities, as the reverie of the poet lying in bed, as a voyage of the human consciousness through vast issues of life and death. It is all these things and none of them." What has happened is that, whereas in other poems differing subjects are treated in order or are mixed, here they are, in the scientific sense of the word, " compounded ", with the purpose not of persuading the reader to this or that but of producing upon him an effect. " La poésie n'a pas le moins du monde pour objet de communiquer à quelqu'un quelque notion déterminée." But " What effect ? " the reader is entitled to ask. " La Jeune Parque ", Dr. Bowra says, " provides an experience." Again the reader may ask : " An experience in what kind ? Was it the poet's intention to communicate his own experience to me ? If so, I am still confused." The answer, surely, is No. The poet's own experience is itself a " notion déterminée " ; his object is not directly to communicate it, not so much to " provide " an experience as to induce in the reader a condition of experiencing. If this be true, the right response to Valéry cannot be an attempt to translate his symbols and apply them, to decipher them and, as it were, write them again in plain language, but so to surrender ourselves to his influence that our own symbolism is enabled and liberated and we also " have a peculiar understanding of matters of great import ".

In comparing " La Jeune Parque " with Valéry's later work and particularly with " Charmes ", Dr. Bowra points out that " the difficulty for Valéry, as for many other modern poets, is to relate poetry to common experience, to find subjects which are neither unreal nor impossibly esoteric, to fuse the findings of the intellect with the visions of the imagination ". This is true, but it is important to emphasize that the difficulty is not inherent in the nature of symbolism itself, but arises, or at any rate becomes formidable, only when there are no longer any commonly accepted symbols and when a poet, feeling unable to use, with certainty of their being accepted, those of Christianity or of classical myth, finds himself in a position corresponding to that of a dramatist who should write for a stage and an audience which had forsaken all the once-received conventions of the theatre.

This point arises again and again in the mind of one who reads Dr. Bowra's book with a desire to relate it to our own world. It is, therefore, worth considering with care. Why is it that men of Rilke's aesthetic purity, of Valéry's intellectual integrity, of Yeats's visionary power, were so often driven into what to the common reader may appear to have been a deliberate obscurity, and how did it happen that Stefan George found himself, at the end, in the position of being acclaimed as a poetical leader by Nazis whose every fanaticism was a denial of the ideal which had been the fountain of his poetry ? And why is it that so many poets of the twenties and thirties, men of deep sincerity and of poetic intuition, gave an impression of writing in chains, in a frustrated agony, as though they were tormented by a kind of spiritual stuttering ? If in the answers to these questions there is a common element, it is a key not only to the internal difficulties of poetry but to the estrangement of poetry from contemporary life.

For a moment, in seeking an answer, let me speak again in terms of the theatre. The power of a dramatist to communicate with his audience greatly depends upon their acceptance of certain conventions — the convention, for example, of stage-time, or the great convention of verse or the little convention of the fourth-wall. The decay of any major convention — that of the chorus or that of soliloquy — is a contraction of the dramatist's power ; his struggle to invent and establish new conventions to replace the old is much more than what is ordinarily called " progress " in the theatre, it is the struggle of the drama to keep touch with its audience, to create and maintain a language generally understood by means of which communication is possible.

Apply this to poetry — above all to poetry which, to employ Donne's great phrase, seeks either to "contract" the " immensities " and so to communicate them, or to induce in us a state in which, as Dr. Bowra says, " we feel that we are the centre, if not of the universe, at least of some enormous scheme, and that anything we do or that happens to us is pregnant with huge issues ". This is made possible only by the use of symbols. The symbols must exercise upon the reader an associative, and so an evocative, power ; they cannot have this power unless they stir within him profound and intimate recognitions. It will be remembered that Baudelaire spoke of " forêts de symboles " which look upon man " avec des regards familiers ". If the symbols cease to be " familiers ", if in the course of less than a century the Christian and the classical symbols recede together in men's consciousness, poetry is deprived of its former means of communication and must discover new. So Rilke invented one terminology and Valéry another ; so Yeats was thrown back upon Irish legend ; so the successors of Yeats, desiring symbols which were not cut off from modern life, went to the machines. But machines are not " familiers " in Baudelaire's sense. By most minds, machines are still seen objectively ; no universal principle is evoked by their name and nature; the "contraction", because it is non-associative, does not embrace or reveal the immensities except in the minds of a few.

This is the central difficulty of modern poets who inherit from the symbolists. The decay of the ancient symbols has imposed upon them the double task of communicating and of establishing a means of communication. Some meet the difficulty by a gigantic struggle to transcend it — Valéry by intellectual penetration, Rilke by a supreme detachment — a rising into the air the better to see the earth as a mapped integration, Yeats by incantation and by the use of legend which happened not to be familiar enough. Another way was opened to Alexander Blok by the special circumstances of his life, and there is no essay in Dr. Bowra's book more exciting than that in which he writes of Blok; for Blok, whose early derivation was from Mallarmé, and who, if he had lived in France, might have had to fight his own version of Valéry's battle, found that the revolutionary changes of the new Russia, which engaged his spirit, threw up, in the minds of the common people, symbols readily accepted and violently associative. George's fate was harder. Though Dr. Bowra is careful not to condemn him, an impression emerges of a man whose desire to regenerate Germany through poetry became a perversion which, before the end, he tragically recognized. The National Socialists tried to adopt him as their own. Dr. Bowra's quiet comment is that, beginning with the ideals of Symbolism, he made " great efforts to translate them into life " and was " in the end content that they should be ideals ". His art " was not the medicine to heal his age ". May we not go further? Art is never a medicine to heal an age. It is " news of reality " expressed in symbols, joys, incantations, enchantments, and the age that cannot read it fails to synthesize its disparate experiences and is "lost in the crowd ".

On Picking
Sides

TO wander through the parks during the summer of
Forty-Three and to find American troops playing baseball there was to remember how, in the golden age, when
rounders was in prospect, nursery-tea had a habit of drag-
ging on, on and on and on, long after you yourself had
eaten all you hoped to eat. Others were slower — girls
for the most part, sisters and female cousins and visiting
daughters of the vicarage — talk, talk, talk, giggle, giggle,
with a piece of cake for ever at their lips, while the lawn
was empty and sunshine waited and you were champing
in your chair.

" Please, may I get down ? "

" Now wait a little, Master Impatient."

Talk, talk, talk. An eternity of knife-twiddling, of the
counting and recounting of cherry-stones. Even when
their cups were empty they would begin to tell fortunes
in tea-leaves. That was too much, an insult to masculine
intelligence. The sense of the House was with you ; you
got down and, though it was more than they deserved,
politely opened the door for them. They streamed out,
downstairs, through the garden, on to the lower lawn,
pledged to rounders. Even then they stood about,
chattering and pushing back long hair from their shoulders,
waiting to be organized. Memory forgives them all their
delays for that matchless gesture of head and hand, that
flow of hair across their fingers. Would that they were
delaying still !

Not that their grace or the game of rounders itself
is a fit subject for a literary essay, but you will remember
that before you could play rounders you had to pick sides.

On Picking Sides

The picking of sides happens to include one of the easiest, and the most easily concealed, vices of criticism, and, if we can be brought to consideration of our vices by way of baseball and the lower lawn, there is excuse (though not much excuse) for the divagation. On the lower lawn the chosen captains picked sides for the oddest reasons : for skill with the stump, for accuracy with the ball, for fleetness of foot — for all these reasons, certainly, and they were good ; for beauty and charm and liveliness — and they were good also, though scarcely scientific ; but sometimes those sides were chosen in plain, wicked partisanship — in conformity, that is to say, with feuds and rivalries and associations that had nothing whatever to do with either the beauty or the fleetness of Atalanta but only with the fact of her being eligible, or ineligible, to a particular domestic clique or club. And criticism, when it has to choose, among the shades of the past, those whom it will recall to the special attention of its own contemporaries, is always in peril of the same naughtiness.

It is among the duties of a critic to recall attention to old writers who have lately been neglected or whose work, he thinks, ought now to be considered in a fresh view. What he will try to avoid, if he can, is the calling-up of great men from the past to serve the purpose of a present and domestic clique. He will not exalt some Caroline poetaster for no better reason than that the verses fit *his* theory of verse-making. Distant writers are to be judged scientifically and to be loved personally, but they are not, without danger, to be conscripted to our little clubs. The distant writer, newly and surprisingly elected to the latest coterie, has attributed to him, by the shrill enthusiasm of its lesser members, virtues not his, while the virtues that genuinely belong to him are glossed over if they happen to be inconvenient to the fashion. Thus, though exalted, he is exalted for the wrong reasons, and suffers a later reaction.

There is some present danger that this may happen to Tennyson. After a long period of neglect he has, in recent years, been recalled to relative favour, but always with the emphatic proviso that what we may legitimately admire is his verse-making, and his verse-making almost alone. He is still represented, so far as his thought is concerned, as a conventionally-minded courtier, a decorative and insincere romantic. There are, in his later work, passages that may be quoted in support of this view, but if there are any ladies and gentlemen inclined to elect Tennyson to their club in the fond belief that he is a tame cat who will be content to purr while they stroke his pentameters, they would do well first to remember in what way he moved his own contemporaries, and to look at his portrait, which is by no means tame, and to read "Maud". It is, indeed, time that the world should re-estimate Tennyson's genius, but let us beware how we elect him to the wrong club — or to any club. His is a genius that will bite.

The Trollopian fashion, which — incredible though it may now seem — coupled Trollope with Jane Austen about a dozen years ago, is worth tracing to its origin. Thirty years earlier, when Trollope was in eclipse, Leslie Stephen wrote an essay on him. While Trollope had been building his reputation, Leslie Stephen had been " one of his devoted readers ". Then his old favourite's charm had fled. One day, at an inn, taking up a book of Trollope's, he found it " as insipid as yesterday's newspaper ", and for long after that " held complacently that Trollope should be left to the vulgar herd ". But by the turn of the century he had " begun to doubt this plausible explanation " of his distaste and wrote a cautious but wise appreciation of Trollope, defending him against Herbert Paul, who had decided that he was dead beyond all hope of resurrection, and quoting Frederic Harrison's

kindlier opinion as a symptom " which might point rather
to a case of suspended vitality ". But Stephen did not
rashly commit himself. He thought, with Frederic
Harrison, that Trollope might have for " our children "
— that is to say, for ourselves — the interest at least of
a singularly faithful portrait of society, but added :

Nobody can claim for Trollope any of the first-rate qualities
which strain the powers of subtle and philosophical criticism ;
but perhaps it would be well if readers would sometimes
make a little effort to blunt their critical faculty. . . . If we
could learn the art of enjoying dull books, it is startling to
think what vast fields of enjoyment would be thrown open
to us. Macaulay, we are told, found pleasure in reading
and re-reading the most vapid and rubbishy novels. Trollope's
novels are far above that level ; and though the rising generation is so brilliant that it can hardly enjoy them without a
certain condescension, the condescension might be repaid.

It was so well repaid that less than thirty years later
Leslie Stephen's daughter, Virginia Woolf, instead of
finding it necessary to blunt her critical faculty in order
to appreciate Trollope, was excusing George Meredith's
imperfections on the ground that they were an inevitable
reaction from " those two perfect novels ' Pride and
Prejudice ' and ' The Small House at Allington ' ".

The immediate consequences of that judgment no one
is likely to forget. Poor Trollope, whose merits so little
fitted him for the part, found himself cast as the literary
exquisite of our late twenties and early thirties. His solid,
story-telling ghost, accustomed to make readers happy by
putting his friendly hand in theirs while he conducted
them from the Great House to the Small House or stood
to watch Phoebus Apollo and Lily Dale on the croquet-
lawn, found himself planted beside Miss Austen on every
fashionable sofa as a pattern of perfection and a reproof
to romantic excess. " George Eliot ", Virginia Woolf
had decreed—

George Eliot, Meredith and Hardy were all imperfect novelists largely because they insisted upon introducing qualities, of thought and of poetry, that are perhaps incompatible with fiction at its most perfect.

But she added, because she wished to find good in the lyrical Meredith as her father had wished to find good in the prosaic Trollope :

On the other hand, if fiction had remained what it was to Jane Austen and Trollope, fiction would by this time be dead.

But is it possible to say, with critical reason, that fiction was any one thing to Jane Austen *and* Trollope ? There were certain things that, to both of them, fiction was not. For example, it was not to either of them what it was to Emily Brontë — an aspect of poetry ; but is that good reason for including them in a bracketed perfection ? The word " perfect ", applied to Jane Austen, is understandable ; it describes her limitation as well as her quality ; she took none of the risks, " of thought and of poetry ", that were perhaps incompatible with her powers, and her genius expressed itself in seeing steadily what she could not have seen so steadily if she had seen it whole.

Trollope also had a gift of avoidance, but in him it was so conventional as to be almost subconscious, while her avoidances were deliberate and selective acts of personal taste ; with the consequence that while her narrative, like the closed heroic couplet, is compensated in " perfection " for the freedom it denies itself, his finds recompense for what Virginia Woolf herself called its " lapses into flatness and dullness " in a rambling, roundabout, talkative good-humour of which the essence is that it is without formal perfection and, at the rate of a thousand words an hour by the clock, made no attempt to strain after it. The result can be seen in Chapter XIV, where a mediocre and tedious passage of Eames's thought is followed by the introduction of a new character, Lord de Guest, masterly in the ease and truth and economy of its dialogue. Trollope had in his boyhood decided that " Pride and Prejudice " was the best novel in the language. To hear " The Small House at Allington " coupled with it in a common perfection would have astonished him as much as it would have astonished Leslie Stephen. And yet, such was his glory in 1928. Now the place beside Miss Austen on the fashionable sofa is unoccupied. Trollope has returned to the company of the imperfect story-tellers, to which, we may hazard, he honourably and contentedly belongs.

There he is probably secure. What led Herbert Paul to clamp down a coffin-lid upon his reputation with so much assurance we can but guess — perhaps, in part, that feminism was then in the air and that the ladies of Barsetshire had not scented it from afar. Such a twist of critical fashion would be no more incredible than the later twist that caused Virginia Woolf to send Trollope and Jane Austen for a walk hand-in-hand over those garden-slopes of Parnassus that are weeded of thought and poetry.

It is by no means surprising, nor is it a reason for self-reproach, that the work of past writers should go out of fashion and return to it again. Men read what interests them and from age to age their predominant interest changes. To complain of this is to complain of human nature. What we have to ask ourselves is whether a critic or anthologist is using, and perhaps distorting, the reputation of a past writer in order to support a case of his own, and whether, conversely, he is suppressing or excluding past reputations because they will not fit into the jig-saw of his personal theory. In this matter, the republic of readers must protect themselves by asking : is this old

73

writer, now suddenly the darling of criticism, being praised for the right or for the wrong reasons? It may be altogether undeniable that he deserves to be praised and that he has been unjustly and too long neglected, but we ought not for that reason to be stampeded into undiscriminating acceptance of the critical-club that has, so to speak, re-elected him.

Questions may, for example, be asked without sacrilege even about Jane Austen herself. Osbert Sitwell has written of " the vulgarity of those who, by the use of a certain coy primness, dream that they follow in the footsteps of Jane Austen ", and it is beyond doubt that the distortion of her just fame has been responsible for a double evil in the contemporary novel : first, for a coy primness, a so-called " perfection " by avoidance, among her devotees, and, secondly, for a reaction towards violence and starkness among those who — again in Sitwell's phrase — take " every stage-elephant, madly plunging in imitation of the real beast, to be genuine ". What links the prim and coy with the stark plungers is their common terror of being called romantic. From the front parlour to the speak-easy, no one, if they can help it, shall accuse them of resembling Turgenev on the one hand or Walter Scott on the other ; and no one does. But as every cult must have a goddess in its own image, Jane Austen has been raised up as an emblem of anti-romanticism, and, while she reigns, let no dog bark. " The big bow-wow strain ", said Scott with charming truth and modesty in praising Jane Austen—

The big bow-wow strain I can do myself, like any now going, but the exquisite touch which renders ordinary commonplace things and characters interesting, from the truth of the description and sentiment, is denied to me.

For justice to Jane Austen we need look no further. She herself might well have replied : " The small lapdog strain I can do myself, like any now going, but the broad sweep that renders heroic events and characters interesting, from the energy of its description and the warmth of its sentiment, is denied to me." But this precisely is what her less balanced adorers and imitators will not say on her behalf. They have elected her to their club for their club's sake, and have sat her down at the door to keep Sir Walter out, for, if Sir Walter got in, they might all be blown off their sociables. But who knows?—perhaps, before long, they may invite him in, on the principle that a shareholder who threatens to become troublesome in independence should be invited to join the board. But they will invite him, if they invite him at all, on their own terms, and discover among his works something — presumably " St. Ronan's Well " — which they can bracket with " Pride and Prejudice " and " The Small House at Allington " as examples of polite, domesticated " perfection ".

It may, in all solemnity, be Scott's turn to-morrow, and George Eliot's the next day, and George Meredith's the day after, to be picked for the side, though how George Eliot is to be purged of the imperfection of thought or Meredith of the imperfection of poetry we can hardly guess. But it can be done. If Trollope can be induced to wear a halo of perfection, anything can be done. " The Small House at Allington " is warm, consoling company on an autumn evening, but — " perfect " ? " Of whom else is it necessary that a word or two should be said before I allow the weary pen to fall from my hand ? " asked Trollope as he dragged on to the last page. He knew what he had written. He gave himself no sea-green airs. A pretty scene appeared to him and down it went — Lily's curtsy, for example :

And then she gently rose up again, smiling, oh, so sweetly, on the man she loved, and the puffings and swellings went out of her muslin.

Perfect ? Yes, in its own kind, and perfect because Trollope did not do what the prim and coy would do : delete " oh, so sweetly " with little scratches of self-consciousness. He marched on — and sometimes found himself knee-deep in mud :

Lily was heart-free at the time and had ever been so. No first shadow from Love's wing had as yet been thrown across the pure tablets of her bosom.

Tablets ? Perfection ? Miss Austen ? . . . In any case, we must take care that Walter Scott, when at last he is allowed to get down from his chair at the immortal tea-party, is not sent in to bat for the Lap-Dogs.

On Being
a Prisoner

LATELY the postman has brought letters from several young prisoners, all unknown or scarcely known to the grateful recipient. " Converse not much with the young, nor with strangers ", said the author of " The Imitation ", in the eighth chapter of his first book ; and the rules of the Kriegsgefangenenpost make it inevitable to obey ; even if one had the handwriting of a Charlotte Brontë or of a calligrapher whose pleasure is to write a chapter within the area of a sixpence, it would embarrass the censors if one were to employ it, and it is undesirable to embarrass these powerful and industrious ladies. How tired they must be of finding that all mankind casts them for the duenna's part and of wondering whether even the rows of amorous but inarticulate crosses beneath a signature are a patterned cipher ! The most innocent truth comes to them with a sidling and self-conscious air. No one attempts to show to them " un homme dans toute la vérité de la nature ". Their existence — however indulgent they may be in their hearts — would be a blight upon Rousseau himself ; and how their ears must ache with the draught of keyholes !

Among the prisoners' letters has been one from Germany, one from Italy, and one from an officer not strictly a prisoner at all except in the sense that upon him also leisure is imposed — a hospital case in the Middle East. All of them write about literature. From that, certainly, no general conclusion is to be drawn. Others, no doubt, are writing about cricket to cricketers or about love to ladies. These three, doubtful perhaps, but wrongly doubtful, of their correspondent's interest in cricket and ladies, courteously addressed him on what, since they had read his books, they knew to be his own subject — and happened to be theirs. They knew also that, in another war, he himself had been a prisoner, and had good reason to believe that, when they said they were writing prose and verse, he would not be astonished or think that they were wasting their time. They were, perhaps, wise enough to guess that he might even be a little envious of them. " Choose for thy companions God and His angels only ", said the author of " The Imitation " in the same chapter, " and flee from the notice of men ". To be a prisoner is to be beyond the notice of men. Though it close doors, it may open windows.

Those whose beloved are prisoners often rely for consolation upon the single thought that they are alive. Their only petitions are that they may not be ill-treated and that some day they may return ; but those who are themselves imprisoned know — or learn after the first shock of confinement — that even imprisonment is not a static interlude in their lives but a part of life itself, full of hazards and graces. Their education by experience has not ceased ; they are lodged in a new school which may permit to them new recreations. Is it not a vanity in us to suppose that only in the company of our freedoms can they be free ? The good in life is deeper than our sorrows and wiser than our complaints. Ask faithful questions always, though as yet the answer be silence.

" . . . So I try now how I can suffer a prison ", wrote Donne in another age and another context, and yet to the point. " And since it is but to build one wall more about our soul, she is still her own Center, how many circumferences soever fortune or our own perversnesse cast about her." This discovery all prisoners make ; it is the beginning of their peril and opportunity. They are driven in upon their " Center ", as we seldom are who butt our heads continually against the circumferences of existence, but who knows what they will find there — darkness or light ? Will their circumferences remain opaque, darkening the " Center " as well as including it, or become translucent so that the " Center " itself is illumined ?

> Or is thy Mind travail'd with discontent ?
> Or art thou parted from the world and mee,
> In a good skorn of the worlds vanitee ?

They are Donne's questions and are applicable to prisoners. Every one has pointed out that life is a kind of imprisonment, but fewer that imprisonment may be a renewal and rediscovery of life.

At first a prisoner is shocked by confinement. He considers his state, not in its own terms, but in terms of the outside world. Yesterday he was free and fighting ; not long ago, it may be, he had leave, and the memory of it is close and warm ; now he is cut off, excluded, cast out, made useless. His mind occupies itself with bitter contrasts ; and a reasonable man, while at this stage of a prisoner's development, often wastes his hours in elaborate protests against his treatment, in bickering about the little privileges of rank, in kicking against the pricks. Or he may become the prey of rationalized fantasy. Rumours torment him continually, he is twisted by grievances against his gaolers or his comrades, he develops an obsession of calendars or ropes or possessions, he hoards and conceals things — all of them, directly or indirectly, emblems of the outside world. Escape, which will afterwards take its place in the perspective of reason, may at first be almost a madness — not a release to be hoped for, a duty to be performed when the chance comes, but a gnawing at the brain that destroys peace and paralyses initiative. But in most men, if their guards do not harry or exasperate them, this phase passes, and many do not experience it at all. Imprisonment is hardest upon professional soldiers, whom it deprives of the chance to distinguish themselves, and upon those whose whole interest in life has hitherto been active. They are, so to speak, world-bound, as ghosts who cannot detach themselves from their former existences are said to be "earth-bound". But even they, except in rare instances, adjust themselves in the end. Their guards say then that a man is "settling down". Donne would say that his mind had ceased to be "travail'd by discontent". But it is, or may be, much more than that.

The change, like the great conversions of ordinary, unimprisoned life, often has small beginnings. The prisoner obtains a pillow a little less hard than that to which he has been accustomed, or he shifts his bed into a position from which he is able to watch the light fall in a way that pleases him, or, raising his hands to his face, he breathes in the odour of some herb that he touched an hour earlier while taking his permitted exercise, and for the first time since he was captured is impelled, by the comfort of that pillow, the beauty of that light-fall, the pleasure of that fragrance, to see the life of prison as a thing of itself, with its own internal proportions and contrasts, and not simply as an exclusion from his former life. This is the first mercy upon prisoners and captives, as it is upon all of us — that by some stroke of life itself they may be awakened to their possession of it and be delivered from hardness of heart.

Next, the prisoner, who had thought that the weeks, the months, the years were being wasted, begins to see time as an endowment. It becomes precious again in its own right. Having lain heavy on his hands, it begins to slip through his fingers. He is delivered from the disgraceful sin of being bored, and begins to cultivate his garden. Again the beginnings may be small. The garden he cultivates — if an indulgent gaoler gives him a little patch to call his own — may be real, not metaphorical, and he, like a child, be drawn into it and find there a companionship of intimate recognitions, so that in the morning he is eager for the hour in which he may be at his garden again and angry when he is called away from it. Or a book may come that casts an enchantment over him, or he may begin to learn an ancient language or a craft, or he may say, as young men have done — and we may smile at but not scorn them — he may say : " I have time enough. I will get my thought straight. I will solve the mystery of the universe." Or he may take up his pen and say to an older man, who might not after all be interested in gardens or ladies or the study of Greek : " I am writing prose and verse. . . . Not with a view to immediate publication. . . ." All these activities — the garden, the Greek grammar, the carpentry, the meditation, the prose, the verse — have this in common : that they are not performed with a view to immediate effect. To the world they are presently " useless ", but they have value. For a young man of our period to discover that what he does is valuable but not useful may be, in many instances, to be born again, and to achieve an undreamed-of tranquillity of spirit. " Heroism and devotion," said Anatole France, " are like great works of art — they have no object beyond themselves." A prisoner may learn this in his prison who might learn it nowhere else.

Anatole France had a queer habit of saying what was true and of failing to grasp the truth of his own saying. His sceptical genius was of the kind, not infrequent among graceful and tolerant writers, that can admit either the air of intellect or the light of intuition but not both at the same time. If he opened a window, he closed the curtains ; not, as some have said since he went out of fashion, because he was shallow and sentimental, but because he was a little timid of catching cold and of being dazzled by the sun. What he would not add, in this instance, is that, though heroism and devotion and great works of art have no object in the sense of looking for effect or reward, though they are arrows without a target in human action or opinion, they are nevertheless not in vain. " Men sacrifice themselves for the sake of sacrifice," he said, and that is true, but he added that the " fatal destiny " of this kind of virtue was " to be always defeated. It gives to its soldiers the incomparable beauty that belongs to the vanquished " — and that is no more than a half-truth. One cannot be defeated if one had no purpose of victory ; an arrow that aims at no target cannot be said to have missed. What Anatole France would not admit is that the value of " useless " devotion or " useless " art is the value of quietism and acceptance, and consists in what it is, not in what it does ; in what it receives, not in what it gives. And it is very hard, in the midst of an active world, to learn the subjective virtue of receiving, but a prisoner may learn it and some day carry at least a part of that knowledge back with him into the world.

The world will have need of it ; so will he ; for it is a virtue we are starved of in every degree of our civilization — in the love of men and women, in education, religion, art. We know how to demand, acquire, capture, not how to receive. Social conscience has taught many how to perform an active service, even how to inspire others, but not how to receive inspiration. We teach love how to charm, to win, to be generous or bold, and say, as if this were the whole art of loving, that the lovers must be wise in their giving and gentle in their demanding ; but the art of submitting themselves to each other and to the inpouring of an essence from outside themselves is little studied. Submission and stillness are thought of as if they were slavishness and a waste of time.

Milton's sonnet on his blindness is read as if it contained but a fourteenth line and as if that were the stale adage of a copy-book. Another blindness, the all-submissive blindness of ecstasy, is strangely abused in the contemporary mind. The great line of Julian Grenfell's — " And who dies fighting has increase " — which some dared to scorn during the long Armistice, was not, as they tremblingly supposed, a praising of brutality in action, but on the contrary a signal, from one who had foreknowledge, that heroism, like art and devotion, is not purposeful, but, being accomplished, is receptive, and has all things added unto it. In that poem there is not a word of victory, of effect upon the enemy. The ecstasy it proclaims is the same in its absolutism with the ecstasies of love and of poetry itself.

> And when the burning moment breaks,
> And all things else are out of mind,
> And only joy of battle takes
> Him by the throat, and makes him blind —

then, because all things else are out of mind, he lies open, the windows are open, the curtains drawn back, the room of his spirit is emptied of earthly purpose, and Day clasps him (it is Grenfell's phrase) and poetry comes to him (it is Keats's) " as naturally as the leaves to a tree ". This we have come perilously near to unlearning and perilously far from wishing to exemplify. There are not many persons who, with the sonnet in their hands, would choose this for to-morrow's sermon :

> God doth not need
> Either man's work or his own gifts.

But to many prisoners it may appear not to have become less true since Milton wrote it.

There is an intolerable sameness in a prisoner's life until he discovers variety within himself, and an intolerable

subordination until he finds refuge in the core of freedom
— the " Center " that Donne spoke of. Having been
taught, as we all are, that in a stormy world it is his
duty to fight unceasingly against the storm and so rise
above it, he is at first tormented by enforced inactivity,
but after a little while he may discover in himself Jeremy
Taylor's skylark which, hoping to get to heaven and climb
above the clouds, was beaten back, and " his motion
made irregular and inconstant,"

till the little creature was forced to sit down and pant, and
stay till the storm was over ; and then it made a prosperous
flight, and did rise and sing

— as if its inactivity had been receptive or, in Jeremy
Taylor's magnificent phrase, " as if it had learned music
and motion from an angel, as he passed sometimes
through the air, about his ministries here below ". Is it
so far a cry from this to the words of the young man who
said from his prison a month ago : " I am writing prose
and verse ", and added with a wry smile : " Not for
immediate publication " ? Are we, who live in masses
and may even be tempted sometimes into thinking of
the effect of our work upon masses, to consider
that he has been made valueless because he has been
deprived of our society ? Is it not well, perhaps, that,
in literature and in life, there should be some who are
given time while they are young in which they may
" sit down and pant, and stay until the storm is over " ?
It is a comment upon the condition to which the activists
and collectivists have brought the world that scarcely
except in prison is this stay possible to the young. Kabir
said that he is the true saint " who requireth thee not to
close the doors, to hold the breath, and renounce the
world . . . who teacheth thee to be still amidst all thine
activities ", and this is true ; this is the supreme self-
mastery to which the long disciplines of wisdom are

directed ; but how shall a man learn it when he is young if he is everlastingly beset, or know even that it is to be learned ? But a prisoner may learn all these things, and in his life or in his literature communicate them, for, though he never address himself to the world, the world is not blind or deaf to a skylark that has "learned music and motion from an angel ". May the prisoner learn how to receive, lest the world altogether forget : accept, receive, submit, lie open, be still. " I am an ambassador in bonds that therein I may speak boldly as I ought to speak."

" La Douceur
de Vivre "

IN the island of Corfu your boat has grounded, you have
gone ashore to swim in that Greek water, and at length
have climbed up from the sunlit curve into the shade
of olive-trees. Did " la douceur de vivre " vanish from
the earth a hundred and fifty years ago ? In the Wye
Valley, the fishermen, bearing their rods between house
and river, are crossing the long-shadowed lawn ; or in
London, in Battersea Park, you watch the stream flow
down between bridges and are suddenly tranquil and
aglow ; or — to meet Talleyrand on his own ground —
you seat yourself, after a journey, in front of a wayside
café in provincial France, and are given coffee and a
" fine ". Did all life's gleam and sweetness fall with the
Bastille ? It is near evening ; the great heat is gone from
the day, the angle of the sun draws a thread of light
downwards, through the stem of the tasting-glass, into
the marble table, cool under your hand ; the time has
come to remember how continuous, how defiant of the
accidents of history, how stubborn against misfortune is
the gentleness of being alive — and how necessary that
it should be valued.

In the imprisonment of routine, in the midst of great
labours, in spite of the temporary inconvenience of
revolutions, men have always known how to let the
instant rest like a petal on the stream of their lives ; they
have loved and painted and written verses and taken a
hand at piquet ; and at café tables or beside a river
they have meditated on these things. Such moments of
reflective ease, while the petal floats by, are not for
Rembrandt or Milton or the giants, assuredly not for

Hugo ; for what is in question is " la douceur de vivre ",
and that is by no means the private property of Titans ;
it is in Tissot and in Fragonard, in the small lanes of
history as well as on the great carriage-routes ; it is a
flower as humble as the willow-herb which is springing up
from nowhere in all the bomb-craters of London, and
has never been reserved to the good and great. And
yet Talleyrand said that only those who had lived in
France before the Revolution had really experienced
" la douceur de vivre ", and, on this theme, Charles
Maurice de Talleyrand-Périgord (1754–1838) knew,
by virtue of his name and period, what he was talking
about.

Lytton Strachey quoted this saying of his at the opening
of an essay on the Abbé Morellet, and Sir Max Beerbohm,
in his Rede Lecture on Strachey, requoted it. Not a
shadow of doubt ? Not a flicker of disagreement ?
Talleyrand we know, and Lytton Strachey we know also
as an authority on eighteenth-century France. In the
first, the saying was natural, a part of his swagger ; in
the second, approval of it was icily unsurprising. But
Max ? At nightfall in his villa outside Rapallo there
would be his own table-talk while dinner continued,
and, after dinner, music from the garden, a singer's
voice drifting in from the Italian darkness. If Max
says, or approves the saying, that there has been no
" douceur de vivre " since the Tennis Court, then
there is no appeal. It is as if Odysseus were to say
that there are no bows or Eros that there are no arrows.
For this is Max's subject — the subject within all his
subjects. He knows as much about it as Talleyrand,
much more than Lytton Strachey, as much, perhaps, as
anyone has ever known since Lesbia's sparrow died. It
is his sense of it that gives to his prose an unsurpassed
mingling of grace with tenderness, so that an essay of
his produces the illusion of sunlit conversation when

it is near evening and the great heat is gone from the day.

What a relief, what a reprieve it is to find that, after all, he offers no endorsement of Talleyrand's sentiment ! He quotes it from Strachey only to show how skilfully that adroit intellect could glide into an essay, and neither agrees nor disagrees with it. It is something, if we are to dispute a little with Talleyrand and to claim that " la douceur de vivre " resides in men themselves and not in their conditions only, to feel that, while the sun shines and conversation continues, there is an open chance of Max's being, in this as in so much else, on the side of the more benign and permissive angels, for there is an alarming array of authority in support of Talleyrand. " The unbought grace of life " — and this is not far from Talleyrand's thought — was believed by Burke to have been extinguished with the life of Marie Antoinette. The age of chivalry, he said, is gone.

That of sophisters, economists and calculators has succeeded, and the glory of Europe is extinguished for ever. Never, never more shall we behold that generous loyalty to rank and sex, that proud submission, that dignified obedience, that subordination of the heart, which kept alive, even in servitude itself, the spirit of an exalted freedom. The unbought grace of life . . . is gone !

It is true that the age of chivalry, as Burke understood it, is gone. We have discovered a different virtue to which the word chivalrous is not altogether misapplied but for which humorous kindliness would be, perhaps, a closer name. Prize the substitute though we may, we delude ourselves if we fail to recognize that not manners and decoration only but a real value, a moral system as well as a polite code, went with what Burke called chivalry. There are many who believe that their loyalty to the post-revolutionary world requires them to repudiate as corrupt or trivial all that preceded it, but this is bad modernism. They might say with greater pride and truer loyalty that they have willingly paid a price for what they have ; that, knowing well how much they have lost, they will seek to re-create what part of it is applicable to the present age.

In any case, Burke's sentences are not to be scouted, even by those who do not, or will not, accept as a real value what he speaks of as " generous loyalty to rank and sex ", for there are other phrases, as always in Burke, which rise up from far below the surface of his or our own prejudices. " That subordination of the heart " says more of the chivalrous principle underlying the manners of chivalry than is at all comfortable for equalitarians to hear, and, though we may justly deny that " heroic enterprise " is dead among us, it is impossible to read of " the unbought grace of life " without reflecting that there is nothing in our own way of living to which it precisely corresponds. Our conduct is by no means so debased as Burke supposed that it must become. The kind of honour which inspires courage and mitigates ferocity is still in the character of fighting-men. Neither " manly sentiment " nor " heroic enterprise " is perished. Nevertheless, the spirit of this conduct is changed. There is not within it that " sensibility of principle . . . which felt a stain like a wound ", but an intuition which is, if you will, more practical, more commonsensical, but is for that very reason the more open to the compromises and inconsistencies of personal judgment. Both we and the pre-revolutionaries have often misapplied our respective ideals. That is not the point. The point is — and it is the residue of wisdom in Burke when his errors of practical estimate have been drained away — that something, some light of being, was snuffed out by the French Revolution. It is lost ; the loss is real ; we are blind if, by different gains, we are prevented from recognizing it.

To this extent Talleyrand was right. But is "la douceur de vivre" among the losses? If not yet, will it soon be?

Enough of it remains to be worth preserving in the face of those whose impulse is to discourage and destroy it — to be worth preserving not only because it is pleasant in itself, a relief from the opposite tedium of merely existing, but because, considered as a social essence, it is a check upon extremists, a spoke in the wheel of "sophisters, economists and calculators", a gracious safeguard against hysterical fanatics. That was one of the reasons for Talleyrand's valuing it so highly. He was an intriguer, certainly; he has been accused of treacherous inconsistency; but there are men who appear to be inconsistent in their following of a particular leader or a particular policy because they so consistently adhere to an overriding principle. Talleyrand was one of these. Look where you will in his career, he is to be seen always firm in two things: a desire for moderation and a lively sense of the impossible. Even after Napoleon's fall, there was a consistency of principle — ironic and even cynical though it may have been — in his labour to save France from the wreck by establishing the rule of legitimacy. Always, when the flames of ambition or enthusiasm leapt up too fiercely, he tried to damp them that the whole house might not catch fire; it is scarcely a reason for calling him traitor that, when these attempts were unavailing, he would sometimes withdraw a little that he might the more comfortably warm his hands. He was fond of money — that is at root the charge against him. The answer is that never for the sake of it did he sell what he believed to be the true interest of France. Given neither to heroics nor to humbug, a man of breeding, taste and intellect, always, it may be supposed, impatient of the Napoleonic vulgarity and bombast, aware always, as few statesmen have been, of something in life itself more unrelenting, more enduring and more charming than the boast and glamour of empires, Talleyrand played his game of politics, knowing it for the game it is. Behind it or within it, he had begun to taste " la douceur de vivre " when, about his thirty-fifth year, the world broke. No wonder he believed that what was gone could have no counterpart. It could have none in his own mind. But that is not to say that it has ceased to exist. As well say there is no poetry that is not written in Alexandrines.

The metaphor is not inapt, for the idea of poetry is interwined with the idea of " la douceur de vivre ", which is the minor poetry of life — the word " minor " being used not in disparagement but as an indication of scale. It is that good in life which is bounded by the words " grace ", " charm ", " quiet ", " gaiety ", " sweetness ", " light ", but does not extend to the vital epic, the ardours and endurances. The territory is restricted — but is wide enough if we remember what meaning was given to quiet at Little Gidding and what Matthew Arnold intended by " sweetness and light ". If we are willing to give this high credit to " la douceur de vivre ", we become entitled to say of our own knowledge that the world did not cease to be capable of it when the French monarchy fell, and that to this extent Talleyrand was wrong. Even elegance, which we are now compelled to omit from our list of defining words, did not vanish with the age he loved, for though, in France, there was a taint of vulgarism in the decorative civilization of Ingres, no one is likely to deny elegance to the Vienna of Chopin's youth or, if it comes to that, to the later Vienna of the Empress Elizabeth. But it is, in general, true that that part of the grace and gaiety which is rightly called elegance faded ; it is lost, we shall never recover it, we can only guess at what it was, and to this extent Talleyrand was right. Let us be unhypocritical enough to acknowledge that the loss is real, and yet have enough confidence in ourselves to say that we have been repaid for it in the sense we have that our civilization is less dependent on the extremes of wealth and poverty than the civilization of Versailles. At the same time, it is necessary to remember that, when Talleyrand spoke as he did, he is less likely to have been thinking of the Court than of the childish years he spent at Chalais. His nostalgia was not for the high decorative refinements of " la douceur de vivre ", which were the privilege, even then, of very few, but rather for those elements of it — grace, quiet, sweetness — which might be experienced by the creatures of an industrial age, even by ourselves, if we knew how to adapt our lives to the experiencing of it.

During the nineteenth century and, with accelerated pace, during the last forty years, this adaptation has become more and more difficult, but there have always been many, in every class of the community, who have been able to make it ; the pressure of mere existence has become heavier and heavier, but has not succeeded in driving all the minor poetry out of life. Even the so-called conquest of the air, which some are inclined to regard as Talleyrand regarded the Revolution, has for the young a lyricism ; they are alive to poetry in machines and have brilliantly received it into themselves. When the world is again a little kind to them and they sit at a wayside café in France, they may — heaven knows ! — feel a song and not a menace in the swarm of gnats overhead. So be it. To every draughtsman the grace of his own line ; to every musician the sweetness of his own instrument ; but however resilient youth may be, however adaptable the spirit of man to changes in its physical habitation, these powers of resilience and adaptation are like all else limited, and, if we are not careful, the time may come when to deny Talleyrand by our own experience may become impossible. " La douceur de vivre " may be trodden out of life — not by suffering or by wars or even by fear and poverty, for all these things it has survived, but by the flat, well-intentioned feet of the civil regimenters, the policemen of the soul, who, whenever a man sits down at a café table or on a bank where the wild thyme blows, are for ever moving him on and considerately offering him a ticket for a youth hostel.

In all the plans that are made for the life we are to lead, how seldom is there evidence of any wish in the planner that that life shall be enjoyed ! That it shall be safe — yes ; that it shall be instructed, rationed, equalized, rubbed smooth, supplied with dustless corners and chromium-plated taps ; but that there shall be grace or charm or quiet or gaiety or sweetness or light in it, there is among the sterner planners neither hope nor desire. Utility and sameness are their guiding stars. Canned milk is their vintage. Their ideal is to make of the art of life what a time-table is to a poem. The word utility, used as a deliberate and waspish denial of men's longing for variety, and held up as a virtue in peace as well as a bleak necessity in war, is the enemy of " la douceur de vivre ". Do you not hear the answer from the bureaucrats — that, in an age of high endeavour, we ought to desire no such thing ! Are we sybarites ? Are we romantics ? Are we not disciplined to the service of the Common Man ? This is the language of their preachment. All their castles in the air are built with glazed bricks for the public convenience. And yet, if we care for democracy at all, it is worth observing that what, in modern times, has distinguished it from the totalitarianism of Right and Left is, precisely, that totalitarian rulers, while industrious in bribing their peoples with bread and circuses, have set their faces against " la douceur de vivre ". Wherefore, unless we desire to conform to their dull and slavish pattern, we do well to accept neither their assurance nor Talleyrand's that the gentleness of living belongs to a past age. Tired men and bureaucrats are for ever saying such things. And this time we have need to beware. Speed and standardization have given to fanatical dullards a means of penetrating the whole life of a people which they never before possessed. They stupefy freedom with gross promises of comfort and security. They speak as if there were neither dancing nor stringed instruments and no sound meritorious on all earth but the scratching of a clerk's pen and the shuffling of a queue. They see the face of mankind only through a guichet. To-day they are unavoidable, and believe that they will always be so. The way to disprove it is to cultivate in spite of them that grace, not of the herd, which fits men to be happy, neither in power nor in possession, when they have made their voyage or fought their battle, and evening comes, with wine or song or hope or memory, and the great heat is out of the day.

Thomas Hardy

IT is not in the least surprising that Lord David Cecil should have written a wise and gracious book on Hardy as a novelist.* His avoidance of whim and pedantry, his concentration on his subject and his will to discern what Hardy was driving at rather than to say what he thinks Hardy ought to have been driving at are consistent with his repute. It is for these qualities that his book will endure as criticism ; and it has another which, though it may not seem remarkable twenty years hence, was so rare three or four years ago that even to-day it gives to a book endowed with it an exceptional air of warmth and sanity — the quality of criticizing a book as a book, a story as a story, a style as a style, and of steadfastly refusing to make literary criticism a platform for sociological debate. " A race of critics has arisen," Lord David says, " who judge a book by how far it expresses what they conceive to be the mind of its period. These people rebuke Charles Lamb for writing in what they call a non-contemporary language. They complain that Mrs. Woolf's novels fail to offer any comment on the significance of modern social changes." In fact, this race of critics is already beginning to edge its way out of the ranks of the stale vanguard in order to change its coat, but its influence lingers among writers of publishers' announcements who still recommend a biography of — shall we say ? — Wordsworth for the light it throws via the French Revolution on the problems of modern Russia. To this race of critics Lord David does not belong. The firmness with which he repudiates them will mean little

* " Hardy the Novelist : An Essay in Criticism ", by David Cecil.

in a future age privileged to forget that they once existed, but is now an encouragement to hope that they will before long cease to exist.

It is, too, a qualification for writing about Hardy. A sociological critic of art, though his whole claim is to modernity, differs little in aesthetic principle from those earnest subjects of Queen Victoria whose judgment of poetry and pictures and novels was continuously influenced by what were then called " problems " ; and Hardy himself, in his weaker mood, when a desire to be up to date tempted him beyond his own range, could entangle himself in a " problem " with unfortunate consequences. A sociological critic, aware of the misfortune, would give as a reason for it that the " problem " was " old-fashioned " or " unreal " — that is to say, a piece of Victorian bric-à-brac, contemptible because it was Victorian, and would miss the point that a " problem " (in the Victorian phrase) or a " social condition " (in our own) is, like everything else, a legitimate subject for art if it stirs the artist's sensibility, if it awakens his aesthetic passion, but not otherwise. Neither " problems " nor social conditions nor morals nor poor ploughmen nor noble dames are, as such, to be ruled out ; but nor are they, as such, to be demanded.

Noble dames did not light Hardy's inmost imaginative fires ; for that reason — and not because noble dames are inappropriate to art — he personally was wrong to choose them as his subject. Galsworthy, for the same reason, was as much at sea when, in his later books, he wrote of the young and smart. He could observe them ; he could — unlike Hardy in the great drawing-rooms — catch, though a little awkwardly, their conversational rhythm ; he could even now and then feel with them, but his imagination's pulse did not beat with theirs, and his sympathy with them, though genuine within the limits of reasoned understanding, did not suddenly overflow those limits and irrigate his knowledge with poetry. It would not be hard to believe that Galsworthy went to cocktail parties with at least a mental note-book, in much the same spirit in which Hardy dined at great houses in order to learn, too late in life, how Lady Mabella walked and talked. And yet not quite in the same spirit, for Hardy, in this as in all else, had a naïveté which made his excursions beyond his range at once more disastrous and less uncomfortable than Galsworthy's. With Hardy it was as if a child were to take infinite pains to gather and bring in a useless weed, supposing it to be a wonderful flower that might delight and astonish the recipient.

Listen to his notion of the conversation of a society débutante at a fashionable London party :

A young friend of Pierston's, the Lady Mabella Buttermead, appeared in a cloud of muslin. A warm-hearted emotional girl was Lady Mabella, who laughed at the humorousness of being alive. She asked him whither he was bent, and he told her that he was looking for Mrs. Pine-Avon. " Oh yes, I know her very well," said Lady Mabella. " Poor thing — so sad — she lost her husband. Well, it was a long time ago certainly. Women ought not to marry and lay themselves open to such catastrophes. I never shall. I am determined never to run such a risk. Now do you think I shall ? " " Oh no, never," said Pierston drily. " That's very satisfying." But Mabella was scarcely comfortable under his answer, even though jestingly returned : and she added, " Sometimes I think I shall, just for the fun of it ! " *

Lord David's comment is that " this is fashionable life as imagined by Miss Daisy Ashford. Lady Mabella is a Young Visiter ", but he is too good a critic to be content with that reproof or with saying what is plain enough and has been said a dozen times before — that Hardy could not give a just impression of the dialogue of Victorian

* The text used by Lord David differs considerably from that of the definitive edition.

aristocrats. He shows — and the passage has been worth quoting for this reason — why Hardy, who must have known that the excursion was perilous, was tempted out of his ground. Here, as always, he criticizes by seeing the subject from Hardy's point of view.

We can see why Hardy chose to write about them. Such people were the inhabitants of the great houses of the Wessex countryside ; and these houses made a real appeal to his imagination, susceptible, as it was, to the imaginative charm of the antique and the picturesque. He wanted to embody his response to them in some story, so he wrote stories about their inhabitants.

To this other possible reasons may be added. It was a weakness in Hardy that he paid too much attention to criticism, for and against. There are instances, in his earliest correspondence with the Macmillans, of his having touchingly quoted from the weekly reviews in support of his own case, and at the end of his life, when experience and a monumental repute might have enabled him to shrug his shoulders, he could still be wounded and provoked to bitter self-defence by a misunderstanding notice of his poetry. A complement to this modesty — or, if you will, to this lack of self-assurance — was his extraordinary willingness to defer to the opinion of those who, he felt, had some kind of right to interfere with his work. Criticism that is hostile or negative, even when it is good and well-founded, is seldom of any use to the artist himself as long as it remains impersonal. So solitary, so perilous, so tender a self-exposure is the practice of art that criticism from the outside, though it may be of use to the world, serves the artist little except when it encourages him to do better what he has already done well. To write, at any rate to write poetically whether in verse or prose, is to open a wound ; it must be touched with love ; if not, the artist recoils from the touch ; it can hurt, but not mend. Therefore, though he can draw good sometimes even from outside criticism, if it be written with a seeing charity and an intuition of his purposes, he relies greatly upon the judgment of one or two whom he loves and who, loving him, know how the child survives in " the great man ", with how little arrogance and how much anxiety he made this or that experiment which has angered a reviewer, and why, in his own terms, he has succeeded or failed, and what, deep within him, and in spite of his defiances, his values are.

This was Hardy's sensitiveness, but a wonderful plainness went with it. Only amateurs — and the word is not used contemptuously but to make a distinction, for there have been great amateurs — only amateurs are impatient or are incapable of being employed. Mrs. Woolf could conform to the requirements of journalism, and Lord David, invited to deliver the Clark Lectures, produced, in this book on Hardy, criticism of the first rank designed for a particular audience. Mrs. Woolf and he were craftsmen and rightly unashamed of it, perhaps even a little proud of their ability to transcend, while accepting, what an amateur might call intolerably restrictive conditions. And Hardy, even when writing his own novels, seems often to have thought of himself as an employed craftsman. If a publisher said that a chapter was too long he shortened it ; if the editor of a magazine asked him to change his ending of a story — even of a masterpiece, " The Return of the Native ", which he deeply cared for — he changed it ; presumably — if he felt it necessary to justify the concession — on the ground that, if an artist of the Renaissance was asked by his patron to add a cow in the foreground, he added it, and if a stonemason at Bockhampton was asked to carve a tombstone in a particular way, he did not refuse. When, after " The Poor Man and the Lady " had been rejected, a more complex story was asked of him, he responded with the thicket of plot-making that is " Desperate Remedies ". It is not at all unlikely that the noble dames were, in part, an honest craftsman's endeavour to supply the market. What in a more self-conscious artist would have been a sacrifice of integrity was often in Hardy but a proof of it. These may be good external reasons for many a lapse into high society — that he was patiently trying to do what was required of him ; or, alternatively, that, in certain moods, he wished to extend his range of character, being too fierily a poet to have Jane Austen's discreet restraints. Praise a man long enough for his milkmaids and he will yearn to write of princesses. But, when all else has been said, Lord David's reason, because it is the reason that springs from the aesthetic impulse, is the truest. Hardy wrote of the great ladies because his imagination, as child and man, had been fired by their houses. This is one of criticism's completely satisfying explanations, directing the artist's own light on a defect and so revealing the defect without detracting from the artist's genius.

Small and relatively unimportant though this question of Hardy's " noble dames " may be, it is valuable as proof of Lord David's sympathy and insight. He does not say in so many words that Hardy had the defects of his merits and that they must be considered as complementary if the novels are to be grasped, but that is the effect of his lectures, which, though they take Hardy in order — considering his range and the limitations upon it, the nature of his art, his power, his weaknesses, his style — combine to give not a diagram but, if one may put it so in speaking of an essay that is not biographical, a portrait of his genius.

The world has outgrown its habit of considering Hardy coarse and impious, but two pitfalls lie in the way of those who wish to grasp his novels as a whole : the pitfall of synthesizing too much, of trying to make a philosophical system out of a series of speculative impulses often contradictory ; and the second pitfall of not understanding to how great an extent his novels are poems, the whole significance of which may be lost by sticklers for rationalism and naturalism and strict consequence.

On the first point Hardy himself insisted again and again. " I have no philosophy — merely what I have often explained to be only a confused heap of impressions, like those of a bewildered child at a conjuring show." And in a letter written at about the same time — the end of 1920 — to Mr. Alfred Noyes, he says :

My imagination may have often run away with me ; but all the same, my sober opinion — so far as I have any definite one — of the Cause of Things (is) . . . that the said Cause is neither moral nor immoral, but *un*moral : " loveless and hateless " I have called it, " which neither good nor evil knows ".

From this, as he points out, it is a long step to the conclusion that the Power behind the Universe is malign, and there are probably few who suppose Hardy to have consistently believed that it was malign. But there may be more who, thinking of Hardy as having been vaguely godless, spring to the conclusion that he was greyly rationalistic, a bleak materialist, without a spiritual, much less a Christian, background to his mind. To believe this is to see Hardy upside-down. If it were true, he could not have begun to write the novels.

I have never understood [Hardy wrote] how anybody can be an atheist except in the sense of disbelieving in a tribal god, man-shaped, fiery-faced and tyrannous, who flies into a rage at the least provocation. . . . Fifty meanings attach to the word " God " nowadays, the only reasonable meaning being the *Cause of Things*, whatever that cause may be. Thus no modern thinker can be an atheist in the modern sense. . . .

And Mrs. Hardy recorded in her biography, as she did so often, Hardy's one deeply illuminating word. He said that though critics had called him Agnostic, Atheist, Immoralist and much else, they had never thought of calling him what they might have called him much more plausibly — " churchy ", not " in an intellectual sense, but in so far as instincts and emotions ruled ".

" Churchy " is a word glorious in its aptness. Combine it with two of Lord David Cecil's sayings and we are brought very near the truth of Hardy in this aspect.

Like many village people, Hardy was always ready to grumble about the vicar. But, taken as a whole, he felt that the loss to human happiness involved in the new scientific interpretation of life far outweighed the gain :

> That with this bright believing band
> I have no claim to be
> That faiths by which my comrades stand
> Seem phantasies to me,
> And mirage-mists their Shining Land,
> Is a strange destiny.

" Mirage-mists " they were for Hardy ; he was not dead to them, but felt them about him. By nature high-spirited, a lover of fiddling, dance and a lilting song, Hardy yet saw life as tragic because his reason, having taken from him his ancestral faith, gave him nothing with which to replace it — not even a palliative indifferentism — but left him emotionally desiring, with a kind of filial passion, what his mind forbade. Lord David gives this truth yet wider range :

The most characteristic note in all Hardy's emotional scale — the strain which, as it were, forms an accompanying undercurrent alike to his scenes of fun and his scenes of tragedy — is nostalgia ; the longing for a world where, if happiness were not really attainable, men were still under the illusion that it could be attained. Nostalgia, gentle in " Under the Greenwood Tree ", lyrical in " The Woodlanders ", romantic in " The Trumpet-Major ", bitter in " Jude ", echoes hauntingly through his every work.

Discover the special tension or the special repose of a work of art and you open the door to the delight and the criticism of it. Nostalgia is Hardy's tension ; a sense of time, as distinct from a sense of modernity, is his repose.

Seen in this light, many of the seeming contradictions of the novels become self-explanatory, and if we remember also the conditions of Victorian novel-writing and the mind of the public to which it was addressed, the unevenness of Hardy's writing — the contrast, for example, between " Far from the Madding Crowd " and " The Hand of Ethelberta " which followed it — ceases to be mysterious. If Hardy had been what many of his contemporaries were — a fighting rationalist, if he had had pride or joy or missionary zeal in his unfaith, his books might have had a flamelike, if arid, consistency. If Victorian novel-readers had been freer of sectarian prejudice — which is not the same thing as moral opinion — or Hardy had been less modestly anxious to conform, as a professional writer, to the requirements of the publishers and editors of his day, he might not have turned so often and with such disastrous consequences from his own tragic and poetic path to become entangled in the vexations of High Society or, even, of society as such. " Seen in the terrific perspective in which Hardy surveys the human being," Lord David says, " man's struggles as a political and social character seem too insignificant to fire his creative spark." Yet sometimes Hardy, saying to himself that he was after all a contemporary novelist and unable or unwilling to assume rank as a Titan, dutifully abandoned his natural perspective and put on eye-glasses of social controversy which were ill-adjusted to his sight. So far, so good. But this is little more than an explanation of his difficulties, of what is erratic in his work. It is of greater interest to dwell upon the qualities

— the dominating tension and the characteristic repose —
which made it great and lovable.

It is among the principal duties, perhaps the first
duty, of a critic to reveal and communicate his own
pleasure in the works of art that are his subject. Lord
David's independence of the fashionable iciness in criticism, his willingness to speak of Hardy with love and
reverence, his power to confess delight without becoming
exclamatory or forsaking reason, inform his book. No
one who reads it is likely to miss the good of Hardy by
approaching the novels from the wrong angle, for Lord
David insists continually upon the fundamental truth of
them : for better and for worse they are a poet's novels ;
that was the impulse and that is the joy of them. Nevertheless their adherence to the story-telling tradition which
was common to Fielding and Scott — the tradition, that
is to say, of plain order and reasonable sequence — confronted their author, who was a poet in a sense in which
neither Scott nor Fielding was a poet, with a rarely
difficult problem of subject and design. Lord David
states the problem in this way :

The novel [he says] proposes to give a convincing picture
of real life ; but, like other works of art, it is only successful
if it composes its material in an orderly pattern. Life, however, fecund, heterogeneous life, is anything but orderly. How,
then, is he to satisfy both his obligations ? How is he to devise
a picture which satisfies us equally as a pattern and as an
illusion of life ? How is he to reconcile form with fact ?

That, certainly, was Hardy's problem, but it is difficult
to go all the way with Lord David in his remarks on
Hardy's treatment of it.

He names Jane Austen as having found a complete
solution. " Her stories are exquisitely shapely and yet
create a convincing illusion of reality."

Not so Hardy. His vision of life was effective enough. Even though it is not a realistic one, it has the profusion and energy of reality. But, in order to force it into a pattern, he tends to impose a plot on it which is not convincing at all.

" In order to force it into a pattern " — is that right ? Does it not presuppose in Hardy a more critically scientific approach to the problem than is at all probable in him ? The problem existed for him, as it does for all novelists, and for him in a peculiarly acute form, but, even though he may have been aware of it in later moods of retrospect and self-examination, he was probably little affected by it, and may even have been unaware of it, while his novels were forming themselves in his mind. The writing of novels is, like the living of life, a strangely unsystem-atized process — not planless, not haphazard, not without care for form and texture, and yet unsystematized in the sense that all planning, all care for form or texture, is subject to the heat of the artist's aesthetic passion, as the most careful ordering of life is subject to the heat of character. He does not " impose a plot " on his vision of life " in order to force it into a pattern ". If he is a natural story-teller in the sense in which Edmund Gosse's mother seems to have been, if he is a man, that is to say, whose mind is fertile of anecdote and legend and who cannot stop telling stories to himself, his choice of plot is very little deliberate ; story after story crowds upon him and his task is to choose one which he can not only feel but write. If he is not a natural story-teller of this simple, ballad-making kind and has to compose his fable, he probably approaches his novel from one of two points far apart : either he begins with a theme, which may at first be little else than an emotion, or with an incident, a phrase, an anecdote from real life, which sets his imagination aglow.

In all these cases, the growth of the novel from its first cause is a double growth. The artist and the craftsman walk side by side. To natural story-tellers, if they are to be believed, the craftsman in them appears sometimes almost as an enemy, as a mentor whose care is, they know, necessary but from whom they are continually tempted to escape. In natural writers, as distinct from natural story-tellers, the artist and the craftsman are more intimate collaborators, but still the craftsman does not " impose a plot " on the artist's vision of life " in order to force it into a pattern ". It is hard to believe that Hardy thought in those terms. What imposed a plot on him — when it was not a publisher or an editor — was the simple fact that he thought in scenes, dramatically, but had not the gift of transitions. His aesthetic passion urged him at all costs to write, for the joy of writing them, the scenes that had sprung up in his imagination ; in them he could do what he most cared to do — discern and communicate the essence of things. Whether they were logically apt mattered not ; they were his truth, his poetry ; in they must go — but he was bad at transitions. His theme was there and excited him ; certain scenes were there, burning to be written ; over all, or within all, were the nostalgia for lost illusions, the sense of man's being a tiny figure in Time's vast landscape, the leaping joy in love and dance and song and good company which clashed always with his frustrate conviction that, though joys were many, happiness was beyond the reach of undeluded man. These, together, were his book. But the scenes — the scenes that burned him — had to be linked, and, when it came to the process of linking, he looked outside himself for help, he learned from Wilkie Collins without caring that he wrote books in a different kind, or, more fatally, feeling in himself that the transitional passages must be dull, tried conscientiously to enliven them. His " imposed " plots — and there is no understanding Hardy until it is understood how much of the industrious apprentice was mixed with his genius — were his attempt to cover the joins. At any rate, so it seems. How Hardy's mind worked we cannot know, but it is reasonable to guess that the awkwardness of some of his plot-making had simpler origins than those Lord David attributes to them.

A difference of interpretation in this matter is, in any case, not to be laboured when discussing a volume that elsewhere penetrates so deeply into the character of Hardy's writing. It has been said that Hardy was a poet using the novel as his medium. What matters is to discern the strength and virtue that were infused into his work by this circumstance and to ask whether or not they outweigh the corresponding technical defects. Much of the theory of the novel and the possibilities of its development depend upon the answers given to two questions : Ought it to be used as a means of poetic expression ? If so, must a new technical method be invented to communicate the poetic impulse or can it be combined with direct story-telling ? It was a custom not long ago to sneer a little at Hardy's novels. They were " melodramatic ", " sentimental ", " stilted ". Only his poetry was said to have enduring value. If that opinion is overruled, and this series of Clark Lectures should do much to overrule it, the modern novel will follow a course radically different from that which it may otherwise take.

Lord David says that the imaginative atmosphere in which Hardy writes of country things does not diminish their " substantial reality ", and quotes Hardy's own view :

Hardy said that the highest art was that which, though changing the appearance of what it describes, only does so in order the better to bring out its essential reality.

Here is the issue. Can the essential reality of a thing or a man or a woman be brought out in a novel of traditional structure ? The answer depends upon what is meant by the " essential reality " of a thing. Evidently in the two phrases used above, " substantial reality " and " essential reality ", the word " reality " is given two different, and indeed opposed, meanings. In the first instance, it is associated with the ideas of " lifelike ", " true on the plane of observation " ; in the second, it means the reality within and behind appearances. This use of one word to mean two things is among the embarrassments of modern criticism. The words " reality " and " realism " are needed for the inmost, the essential reality ; " natural truth " and " naturalism " might be allowed to serve on the plane of sensuous observation. If this were accepted it would be possible to say without fear of being misunderstood, that Hardy brought out the essential reality of things by changing, by intensifying, their appearances on the naturalistic plane. Not only is it true that what he gives are pictures, not photographs, but true also that his pictures are deliberately stylized. Description and dialogue alike are saturated with his style — a style so gnarled, so startling in its emotional grandeurs, so queer in its sudden muted formalities, that its effect is that of poetic incantation ; it puts the reader under a receptive spell, in which state Hardy can do anything with him. The style is used — who can say how deliberately ? — to break down resistance, to suspend disbelief.

How successfully it was used can be seen in the effect it had on Lord David himself, who observes grave structural flaws in the later chapters of " Tess ", where, he says, the novelist's " lawless imagination . . . bolted with him " :

He brings Alec back into her life, unconvincingly disguised as a Revivalist preacher. Then he would have us believe that Tess goes back to him in order to get money to support her poverty-stricken family — though she could more easily have got money from Angel's relations. Finally, Angel comes back, penitent for his heartlessness and willing to forgive her. She flees with him, but makes use of the few moments before she starts to murder Alec with a breakfast knife, with the result that she is shortly afterwards arrested and hanged at Winchester. This last section of the book is imagined with such intensity that, on first reading, it sweeps us off our feet. But a cooler perusal begins to shake our faith. Why on earth should Tess murder Alec if . . .

But it is too late to ask that question ! There happens to be a good answer to it for a reader of " Tess " who disagrees on that point — the answer that Tess (who knew about Hardy's nostalgia for lost illusions) desired to kill in fulfilment of the life denied her. But the answer to that question is not the point. The point is that Hardy by his genius has made it too late to ask it. " On first reading, the passage sweeps us off our feet." Is not Hardy's purpose accomplished — the purpose to write with such intensity, with such poetry, that disbelief is suspended, resistance broken down, and the " essential reality " brought out ? In him an improbability that breaks the illusion is a fault because his feet at any rate are on earth and he must obey the rules of earth, but an improbability — if it is one — of which the reader is unaware until a later analysis, beyond the poetic spell, reveals it to him, is, surely, to be regarded less as a fault than as a difficulty transcended ?

Hardy's strange power to communicate the essential reality of a thing by the intensity of his story-telling and by the wild, unhesitating splendour of the phrases he could make shine in a formal setting was applied to everything. Not only did he exhibit the spiritual essence of a man or a woman by this means, but he penetrated the appearances of nature — of wood or moor, of darkness or sunshine — and could persuade his reader to feel the impact of beauty itself or of innocence itself while seeming only (in the tradition of plain story-telling) to be busied with the description of a beautiful face. Lord David points out that Thomasin, in " The Return of the Native ", is tender and faithful and timid, " just like a heroine in the Waverley Novels. But they are insipid ; and she is not. His poetic faculty enables him to suffuse her personality with the innocent, romantic grace which was her attraction." And he quotes Hardy's description, which is worth examining :

A fair, sweet, and honest country face was revealed, reposing in a nest of wavy chestnut hair. It was between pretty and beautiful. . . .

Nothing yet to take the breath away and nothing for a little while. Then a sentence of stiffness, almost of awkwardness, characteristic of Hardy when his imagination was crouching to spring :

The scarlet of her lips had not had time to abate, and just now it appeared still more intense by the absence of the neighbouring and more transient colour of her cheek.

Certainly, the reader says, no one but Hardy could have written that. Its observation is accurate and firm, but "abate " — is not that a little stiff? And "neighbouring " — is not that redundant ? And yet " abate " is the right word and has an appropriate dignity, and " neighbouring " is intuitively redundant. It is there to slow the rhythm. For now the poet is to strike. A short, intermediate sentence — then " the essential reality " :

The lips frequently parted, with a murmur of words. She seemed to belong rightly to a madrigal — to require viewing through rhyme and harmony.

" She seemed to belong rightly to a madrigal." There is Thomasin within and beyond the appearances of Thomasin.

Wherever one looks in the Wessex Novels, except when Hardy is working clean outside his range, the same power appears. His greatness consisted in being able to tell a story at least reasonably enough not to prevent an admirer of Jane Austen from being swept off his feet, and, at the same time, to " bring out the essential reality of a thing ". " I don't know whether that is what I look like," he said once of a portrait of himself, " but it is certainly what I feel like." Any one of the great characters of his novels might, with equal truth, say to the reader : " I don't know whether that is how you expected me to behave, but that certainly is what I am."

An Expectant
Silence

IN America, during the three months that preceded and
the six that followed Pearl Harbour, I was asked continually what effect the war had had, and was likely to have, on
the literature of England and particularly on our poetry.
The first thing to notice is that the question was so often
asked. Those who suppose that the Americans are, at
root, a materialistic people are grossly deceived, though
there does lie upon parts of their civilization a hard
veneer. It is true that, in them, the tendency of all
numerical democracies to estimate value by quantity —
to be impressed, for example, by the sales of a book or
the income of a man — appears to be more pronounced
than in ourselves ; the word " dollar " is more frequent
in their conversation than the word " pound " in ours ;
they fall more easily than we under the spell of statistics
and are much more swiftly diverted from one opinion to
another by the pressure of what is, or what represents
itself as being, a majority opinion. Not only politicians
and film-actors, but men as deeply established in the past
as Edgar Allan Poe, come in and go out on the tides
with a rapidity that would astonish in England even
those critics who periodically consign Tennyson or Wordsworth to the purgatory of their disregard. In America
any quiet immortal may surprisedly awake one morning
to find himself infamous, and the same volatile temperament, the same love of enthusiasms for their own sake,
which makes this possible, makes Americans impressionable in other things, so that " record " speeds or outputs
or fortunes are not only good headlines but produce a
feeling of solemn respect in many minds. But this tend-

ency to enthusiasm does not apply to money or success alone ; it applies to everything — to religious movements, for instance, to educational experiments, to blue-prints for the reorganization of society, even to poetry. As long as we recognize in ourselves the opposite peril of a lack of warmth, a too indifferent scepticism, we may reasonably say that American enthusiasms are sometimes uncritical, but not that they are materialistic. It follows that any persistent American questioning is relevant to an attempt to reassess our own values.

What, then, has lain behind American curiosity for our literature since the autumn of 1939? An intuitive knowledge that the truth of a country is in its art, not in its polemics, and a desire to know the truth. Though our resistance to aerial attack after the fall of France had done much to raise our stock in the United States, the idea that this was a " phony " or at any rate an obscurely different war persisted to the end of 1941 and beyond it. The last war had .produced at once Brooke, Grenfell, Robert Nichols and, later, in a different mood, Sassoon — an outburst of song, heroic, romantic or caustic ; the older men, Hardy, Kipling, Housman even, had resumed their instruments ; Mr. Britling had been volubly prepared to see it through. This time, to the American ear, silence. Why? Did we believe in nothing, that we sang of nothing? Had we no hope, that our poets expressed none? Or was this war so different in its nature from other wars that artistic response to it must necessarily be deferred? The questions were, perhaps, over-simplified, the negative assumptions upon which they depended too sweeping. Any Englishman who wished to do so could then, and čan still, bring forward honourable instances of verse and imaginative prose that have sprung from the war, but the Americans, if they had ever heard rumours of them, had forgotten them. That they had forgotten is the point to be remarked. "The White Cliffs" and "This Above All" were being read from New York to San Francisco with a lively sense that they were inadequate. Even Americans themselves, living in England and loving her, had produced nothing memorable. Where was Henry James? Where was Brooke or any counterpart of Brooke? Where, indeed, to drop back across time, was Wordsworth? Where, if it came to that, was Huxley? Had Auden nothing to say?

When every allowance for exaggeration has been made and every exception quoted, the silence, it must be acknowledged, is conspicuous. Americans reject with justice and reason all materialistic explanations of it — the empty plea that artists are otherwise occupied, or the worse one that this is an economic war being fought in an economists' age and that there is, consequently, nothing to sing about. Attempted explanation must strike deeper than that. The interval between wars holds the key to many contemporary problems, and there it is worth while to look for the key to this.

More than twenty years ago Hardy published, with his "Late Lyrics and Earlier", a highly controversial preface. "Some of his friends", Mrs. Hardy has told us in her biography, "regretted this preface, thinking that it betrayed an oversensitiveness to criticism which it were better the world should not know", and she added that "an interesting point was his attitude towards religion", he having seemingly hoped — a strange hope in Hardy, if Mrs. Hardy's account truly represents it — that the revision of the Prayer-book then being discussed would make "the Established Church comprehensive enough to include the majority of thinkers of the previous hundred years who had lost all belief in the supernatural". Is it possible that a man so ironic and so little sanguine

as Hardy can have hoped for that ? His own words seem
hardly to support his biographer's interpretation :

It may indeed be a forlorn hope, a mere dream, that of an
alliance between religion, which must be retained unless the
world is to perish, and complete rationality, which must
come, unless also the world is to perish, by means of the inter-
fusing effect of poetry. . . .

This is a far step from reliance upon a changed Liturgy.
In any case, for us, the significance of the preface lies
not alone in this passage to which Mrs. Hardy drew attention but in a prophecy linked with it which stretches
out towards our own times for refutation or fulfilment.

It is almost a cry of despair for English literature.
" The thoughts of any man of letters concerned to keep
poetry alive cannot but run uncomfortably on the pre-
carious prospects of English verse at the present day.
. . . And a forward conjecture scarcely permits the hope
of a better time, unless men's tendencies should change."
This is the least of it. " All art nowadays " is included.

Whether owing to the barbarizing of taste in the younger
minds by the dark madness of the late war, the unabashed
cultivation of selfishness in all classes, the plethoric growth of
knowledge simultaneously with the stunting of wisdom, " a
degrading thirst after outrageous stimulation " (to quote
Wordsworth again), or from any other cause, we seem
threatened with a new Dark Age.

It is so terrible a spiritual indictment that the impulse
of many readers was in 1922, and may still be to-day,
to brush it aside with the old, stubborn exclamation that
Hardy was " a pessimist " or that he had " no sense of
humour ". To say this of their prophets has before now
led peoples to their complacent ruin. It is better to
inquire, while there may yet be time, whether the
question of our artists' silence or inadequacy is not, in
essence, Hardy's question, and whether his prophecy is

or is not being fulfilled in our literature on both sides of the Atlantic.

Hardy spoke, as he admitted, "somewhat sweepingly"; he was bound to "except many thoughtful writers in verse and prose"; so are we, in retrospect. Nevertheless, his condemnation of the period in which he wrote stands. The twenties and the succeeding thirties, even when brilliant, were arid, valuable chiefly as periods of transitional experiment. Insist again on the exceptions — Yeats, let us say, though Yeats himself passed through a phase in which, over-anxious to range himself with younger men, he embarrassed his own Muse in teaching mannerisms to theirs. They themselves were restricted by a deadly fear, then disguised as a boldness — the fear of not escaping from the forms of the past, or, in Virginia Woolf's phrase, of not scraping themselves "free from certain falsities, the wreckage of the great Victorian age". And fear, above all of singing too much or loving too much, is a weak motive for poetry. It drove the poets who suffered from it into a seclusion so narrow that they could find there nothing objective to describe, no humanity external to themselves, and, when they looked inward, "not the self that loves a woman, or that hates a tyrant, or that broods over the mystery of the world" (for were not these Victorian subjects?), but only a world that had "no existence except for one particular person at one particular moment". The result was obscurity of a special kind, not the obscurity which arises, in great poetry, from the fullness of the subject and the divine compressions of language, but a house-party obscurity, an affair of nicknames and tittle-tattle, difficult even within the coterie, meaningless — and intended to be meaningless — outside it. Nevertheless, these poets had value as a purge, and one outstanding merit — that they were not glib. They may have been marking time in a dusty barrack-square, but at any rate they gave the camp-followers of Victorianism time to die. Meanwhile, aware that they were walled in and cut off from this man or this woman in the street outside, they struggled to compensate themselves for so barren an isolation by setting up as laureates of the masses. " But it is October, 1931," wrote Mrs. Woolf, " and for a long time now poetry has shirked contact with — what shall we call it ? — shall we shortly and no doubt inaccurately call it life ? " This, coming from her whose whole attitude towards modern experiments was different from Hardy's, is confirmation, offered in mid-channel between the two wars, not of his prophecy but of his diagnosis. Together they explain the silence that fell in 1939.

It is the silence not of death, for poetry is among the constants, not even, perhaps, of Hardy's " Dark Age," but of suspense. The men of the anti-romantic, anti-Victorian, de-humanizing purge have done their work and closed the bracket. If, as seems possible, they have cleared the way for a poetic restatement of life in terms of spiritual value, if rhythm is to rise from their dust and sing new songs, if the cause of the silence is that time is needed by them or their successors " to re-think human life into poetry ", they will have served their turn. Their extreme, bracketed aridity was, perhaps, required not only to kill off the post-Victorian weeds but to compel a fresh impulse in the tradition from which they departed.

So we are driven back to the question that American students ask with such pertinence and ardour — what is the direction of that impulse likely to be ? The readiest answer is : " It depends greatly on you ", but a visiting Englishman is not allowed that easy avoidance ; he must make his prophecy or perish. One approach to the question may at any rate be attempted by saying that what appears to be vanishing from the work of young writers in America and England is a double motive to

which their immediate predecessors have been firmly
wedded — the motive of self-pity and of the direct imputa-
tion to others of blame for all their woes. By self-pity
I mean here an angry and political self-pity, a barren
motive to be carefully distinguished from the individual-
ized sadness of Keats or the passionate solitudes of
Leopardi. The young men of yesterday had too often
an air of grieving narrowly because someone older than
themselves or of a political party different from theirs
had cruelly let go of their hand on a dark night.

> Around, around the sun we go :
> The moon goes round the earth.
> We do not die of death :
> We die of vertigo,

wrote Mr. Archibald MacLeish seven or eight years ago
in justifiable satirical comment. Young poets of to-day,
though their manner differs from Leopardi's, are often
astonishingly near to him in spirit. " So youth from us
is taken " (the translation is from Mr. Geoffrey Bickersteth's scholarly volume), " Even so it leaves forsaken
Our mortal years."

> Tal si dilegua, e tale
> Lascia l'età mortale
> La giovinezza. In fuga
> Van l'ombre e le sembianze
> Dei dilettosi inganni. . . .

All over the United States, as those who read the under-
graduate magazines must be aware, and in England
also, though here the liberation has been slower, young
men, feeling that they have grown suddenly older and
that (to pursue the Italian poem) the hopes they once
cherished have receded from them, are struggling to
express in their own idiom an acknowledgment of the
truth, which is neither weakly resigned nor pettily
rebellious. They seem to be recovering what, in Hardy's

" Dark Age " of literature, seemed to have been lost —
a sense of Destiny which, while it makes no man less
responsible for his own life, gives him a dignity beyond
mere whining.

The conclusion to be drawn is assuredly not that the
future will be romantic in the sense in which Leopardi
— a little hesitantly if we consider him deeply enough —
may be said to have been romantic. Mr. Bickersteth, in
writing of Leopardi, has pointed out that he was " the
junior of Byron by ten, of Shelley by six, and of Keats
by three, years " and that the year of his birth was that
of " Lyrical Ballads ". It is a significant note. The
direction of the artistic impulse in the years to come may
be determined by a single book, as it was then by " the
little volume " of Coleridge and Wordsworth, or may
be a consequence of the accumulating pressure of men's
revolt against the loveless, timid and jealous convention
which has for several years, under the command of a
group calling itself " modern ", made war against all
poets who felt or sang as individualists. " Turning from
the Georgians to the moderns," Mr. Cyril Connolly has
written, " we abandon the lyrical for the intellectual, for
the poetry with a frown." All we may be sure of is that
the new flowering of English poetry, when it comes, will
be unafraid of this frown of ageing governesses, and that
it will not be, in the aggressive sense of the twenties and
thirties, anti-romantic. The poets are remembering that,
in literature as well as in life, self-conscious " youth movements " are a falsification of values — an extremely
spurious form of romanticism. They are beginning to see
that to be old is only to have been young ; that to love,
though its consequence be suffering, is not to be ridiculous ; and that to " die of death " is saner than to " die of
vertigo ". The bleak severance of past from future is over.
Memories and dreams have ceased to be dishonourable.
" Vaghe stelle dell' Orsa, io non credea. . . ."

> Lovely stars of the Bear, I never dreamed
> That I should e'er again, as in old times,
> Gaze on you glittering o'er my father's garden . . .

But it is not impossible. There is evidence of nightingales.

The
Abbey

HE is the surest friend who does not change with the
seasons of fortune, but

> . . . is an ever-fixed mark,
> That looks on tempests and is never shaken.

It is true, as Shakespeare intended it, but there is a
dependent truth — that a friend's constancy changes its
aspect in accordance with our needs : he is the sunlight
of our happiness, our shade in the heat of the day, the
fair wind of our setting-out, the harbour of our storm-
driven return. It is not that he adapts himself, as
flatterers will, to our prides and frailties ; nor is he our
tutor to admonish them ; but his steadfastness has the
miraculous quality of a work of art in which, at each
approach, we read ourselves anew, and which, by its
compassion with our mortality, enables us to distinguish
our greeds from our necessities, our shrill complaints from
the profound and reconcilable griefs of the soul. The
quality is not of changeableness, not even of adaptability,
but of " ever-fixed " response — an unfailing power, not
merely to receive, comfort and assuage those who travail
and are heavy laden, but to refresh them : that is, to
make possible their rebirth. It is the supreme, the
essential quality of love. It is the essential quality of
art, distinguishing it from all masqueraders. And it is
the quality which, above all others, has made of Westminster Abbey, for men of our race, a building unique
in the world.

Go there on an afternoon of this fifth winter of war.*
It is Sunday. Outside, a bleak drizzle is falling on the

* First published on New Year's Day, 1944.

half-deserted streets. Many of those who now enter by the west door might not have gone in but to shelter from the increasing rain ; others, strangers to London, strangers to England, have come, under the ancestral impulse or, it may be, the impulse of curiosity, to "see the Abbey". For whatever reason they have come, with however casual an intention to look in and be gone, the Abbey holds them, holds us all, empties out our preoccupations, quiets the differences and cancels the strangenesses of men who speak the English tongue — even that false, artificial estrangement, which has cursed our century, of youth from age. To some of us the scene is a part of our earliest years. Our eyes move first to what, for them, must always have the unfamiliarity of newness, to the grave of the unknown warrior, for example, beside which, gathering, standing, slowly dispersing, is a continuous group of young men and women in uniform, whose childhood sprang, as it were, from this memorial grave and who are come now to redeem it. We of an earlier regiment, whose companion in arms may lie buried there, watch them at first with a sense of their being divided from us, but division fades where the kings lie down together and, in them, their unremembered servants. The generations of men are reconciled, not, as the harsher moralists have said, by a common abasement to which death compels them, but by a liberation and welling up of their common humanity, which overflows the banks of age, faction and blood, and sweeps across the interval between the living and the dead.

The afternoon Service is ending. For a little while an assembly of fighting-men and civilians waits at the barrier, looking in upon the shadowy congregation and the lighted altar. When the barrier is taken down, they flow on into the transepts, to the poets in the South or to the statesmen in the North, seeking, it would appear, in many instances, some monument that they have previ-

ously decided to visit. They find it, read the inscription
stand there for a time — then, turning away, hesitate,
are at a loss ; but their being at a loss for a particular
direction becomes at once their opportunity to discover
the whole Abbey, to feel its response, to be received into
it, and they move henceforth with as lively and tranquil a
wonder as a man has in a wood which, in youth, was his
own, and is now both deeply familiar and half-forgotten.

Even by those of us who have had most opportunity
to learn it, how little is the Abbey known — or, rather,
how well, how intimately, but how inaccurately ! In
this it resembles a great and beloved book that we have
read again and again until it has become so interwoven
with our experience that we could by no means pass an
examination on it. What is the book's detail ? What its
plot ? What precisely will happen as we turn the corner
from chapter nine to chapter ten ? Some are able to
carry all these things in the forefront of their memories ;
it is their way of honouring a masterpiece ; but there is
another way — that of the mind which frees itself after
each reading from memory of the parts, to retain, perhaps
the more lovingly, an impression of the whole — a sense
of personality, of style and rhythm, of emotion : that
distinguishing tang of being, of essential life, which marks
a great book or a human creature in its uniqueness.
This way of remembering — or, if you will, of forgetting
— a book or a friend preserves an everlasting freshness
of re-encounter. What is forgotten is the mechanics that
are staled by repetition ; what is guarded is the distillation of a work of art or of a human presence which,
because it is for ever responsive to the variety of our own
need, age cannot wither nor custom stale. Do we know
a picture the less because we cannot recall whether the
right hand of the sitter was folded upon the left or the
left upon the right ? Or a friend because we have forgotten the colour of his eyes ? Or the Abbey because we

could not draw its plan and might at any moment be at a loss in it ?

What matters in the act of memory is not order and completeness but a springlike vitality of impression, not the bleak catalogue of photography but the ever-fresh and ever-wonderful impact of portraiture. To know anything completely is to kill it. So the human mind kills little books and shallow loves and the trivial gods, sucking them dry until they have no more to give and are even incapable of receiving. There are minds so pre-datory, so murderous of faith, that they would, if they could, suck all experience dry in the same way ; and it is the quality of greatness in all great things — in books, in love and in the gods — to defy human acquisitiveness, to outrange our knowledge, to transcend our finalities, reserving within themselves that area of the unknowable and unseizable which is the window to all our prisons.

It is in this sense that the Abbey is not to be learned, captured or tamed. To every man who has not hardened his heart against it and is of our race, it reveals itself as an unbounded extension of his own imaginative life. As he stands within it " at a loss ", feeling himself, it may be, a stranger here, an exile in a foreign city from his home beyond the seas, it becomes — as the expression on many a face proves again and again — mysteriously personal to him, full of recognitions and remembrances, and exhibits the day through which he is now living, the instant in which he is drawing breath, not as an imprisoned and bracketed present, locked in by war or loneliness or the blind pressure of society, but as a movement in his own experience — not a happy one, not lighted even by any close expectation of happiness, but nevertheless a movement, a flow, a communication, a means of life, an acceptance, not a frozen rebellion or an inhibited despair. This is the Abbey's " ever-fixed " response to personal need. There is none to whose vision of life, blurred by too close a self-regard, it will not give perspective, restoring sight to the spiritual eye.

This power of the Abbey Church of St. Peter to refresh the spirit of private men — a power the more gracious because it is shared by much humbler churches, each in its own manner and degree — has been less remarked than its more conspicuous quality of representing the history and character of our race. It is the fact that the two qualities — the personal and the historical — are here combined which gives to the Abbey so lovely an expression of tenderness with grandeur — a tenderness more austere than that of certain small churches in England or France or Italy that each one of us has found for himself and treasured in his heart as his especial refuge, and, at the same time, a grandeur less superb, less dwarfing to our mortal stature, than that of Chartres, the most beautiful of cathedrals. The tenderness and the grandeur of Westminster marvellously temper each other — perhaps for the reason that the grandeur itself is not only or chiefly architectural but, in the noblest sense, derivative from the fallible greatness of the English peoples. Even our follies, our prides, our disproportionate estimates of human worth are all visible in that forest of monuments, and yet are pardoned by the Abbey's power to transcend them. In the end, the impression that remains is of a maternal grace, at once proud and compassionate, which suffers the children of England to leave their toys lying about because they have been justified in their spirit. Of that spirit the Abbey itself is almost a definition, but a definition hard to put into words. We may appropriately turn for aid to a great American who happened to come very near the truth in an essay on an Abbey-burial.

On the last day of the year, a little more than half

a century ago, there was buried at Westminster one who seemed to many of his contemporaries an intruder. Three weeks earlier, on December 12th, 1889, he had died at Venice, and now " received, in the direction of becoming a classic, the only official assistance that is ever conferred on English writers ". The words are Henry James's. He himself had no doubt of Browning's title, but was aware that others might deny it.

A good many oddities [he said] and a good many great writers have been entombed in the Abbey ; but none of the odd ones have been so great and none of the great ones so odd. There are plenty of poets whose right to the title may be contested, but there is no poetic head of equal power — crowned and recrowned by almost importunate hands — from which so many people would withhold the distinctive wreath.

The difficulty, as Henry James saw it, was Browning's extreme modernness, by which he meant " the all-touching, all-trying spirit " of the poet's work. This, he suggested, would give " the marble phantoms something to puzzle out, until——" and here he recognized the Abbey's extraordinary power of assimilation, of reconciling the new with the old

— until, [he continued] by the quick operation of time, the mere fact of his lying there among the classified and protected makes even Robert Browning lose a portion of the bristling surface of his actuality.

How strangely, now and then, does Henry James mar the excellence of his discernment by twisting a phrase a little too far towards an almost dandified irony ! " The classified and protected ", he says, as if they had been admitted to an exclusive club. Would it not have been simpler and truer, in writing of the Abbey, to have chosen the plain word : " received " ?

But Henry James, though he was, perhaps, a little too anxious not to risk a charge of having been over-

impressed by the Abbey Service which he had attended
" on Tuesday last ", had the truth of Browning in him
and, in expressing it, expressed much more. Browning's
voice, he said,

sounds loudest, and also clearest, for the things that, as a
race, we like best — the fascination of faith, the acceptance
of life, the respect for its mysteries, the endurance of its
charges, the vitality of the will, the validity of character, the
beauty of action, the seriousness, above all, of the great
human passion.

How near does New England come to us in that passage !
How the history of our race rises up as the history of
our adherence to, or our swerving from, that set of values !
What a fiery questioning they confront us with to-day,
for now it is not one or two or three that are challenged,
as they have been in gentler periods of our history, but
all — the whole foundation of the good in us, the whole
justification of our spirit, our whole chance of being
pardoned, in history's final reckoning, for having so often
left our toys about ! And if we would learn of those
things anew, and match ourselves as we now are with
what we believe to be the ideal of our race, we may
find in the Abbey that ideal embodied and eloquent. In
writing of "the things we like best" — that is to say,
of the values that we intuitively rank before all others
— Henry James was describing, almost, it would seem,
without knowing what he did, the character of the Abbey
itself. At the head of his brilliant list stands the fascination of faith and, near the end of it, the beauty of action.
They are the tower and the foundation of Westminster,
and between them lies the whole teaching of her stones.

It may be observed that, among the rewards now
offered by materialists to the inhabitants of their new
world, none of the things which, Henry James says, we,

as a race, like best is ever mentioned. Many of his values are deliberately and scornfully rejected. "The acceptance of life, the respect for its mysteries" can have little attraction for an all-knowing populace, and, as for "the endurance of life's charges", is not the need for any such thing to be lifted from us by an all-provident bureaucracy? Continue to read the list item by item. The emphasis is always on being, not on having; on duty, not on rights; on the "seriousness", not on the appetite, of passion. It is not an easy creed. Even the absence of · war, which we are now urged to claim as a supreme right, is not advanced as one of "the things we like best" — perhaps because in the first days of 1890 Henry James took it for granted, but perhaps because he was historian and philosopher enough to perceive that war is a symptom, not a disease, that it cannot be cured except in curing the whole spiritual state of the body politic, and that meanwhile it is among the "charges" of life to be endured. All this is heresy to those who teach that the purpose of living is to live easily, and that, when life has not been made easy for him, man has cause for bitter complaint. No one who stands in the Abbey, considering it either in its Christian or in its memorial aspect, can long continue to believe that the flatterers of his materialism speak truth. His grievances become less important to him than the validity of his character, his desires than the vitality of his will, and as he moves forward among his inheritance he becomes aware of how profoundly he is insulted by those who with the bribes of comfort and pleasure would seduce his integrity. For whether he be Celt or Norman or New Englander, whether his own people be of the included or of the issued sovereignties, the Abbey, which the Normans themselves in the newness of their power honoured for the Confessor's sake, is his by the right of his forefathers, and within its walls he is not a separated man, a vain law unto himself, but a member of a great company, by whose law he is protected and bound. And the law is plain. It is of compassion and justice, which we in our generation do, indeed, strive after, but it is a law also of inalienable responsibility, personal in being and in action, not to be delegated or divided or postponed. The acceptance of life means the acceptance of its requirement with its privilege, each as the complement of the other, so that we do not kick against the pricks or set ourselves up against the gods. We stand between our forefathers and our sons' sons. Of ourselves we can do nothing. Our life, as the Abbey teaches, is a means of life, a communication between a faith and a wonder.

Emily
Brontë

IT is Friday evening near 9 o'clock — wild rainy weather.
I am seated in the dining room, having just concluded
tidying our desk boxes, writing this document. Papa is in
the parlour — Aunt upstairs in her room. She has been
reading " Blackwood's Magazine " to Papa. Victoria and
Adelaide are ensconsed in the peat-house. Keeper is in
the kitchen — Hero in his cage. We are all stout and
hearty. . . .*

This is the opening, written on her twenty-third birthday, of one of the few pieces of directly biographical
material that have come to us from Emily Brontë. There
are two stiffly formal letters from her to Charlotte's friend,
Ellen Nussey ; there is the " document " from which I
have quoted, written on July 30th, 1841, as part of a
scheme, arranged with Anne, whereby each should set
down her summary of four years past and her forecast
of four years to come ; there is this document's successor,
dated 1845. That time will reveal other letters of hers
is scarcely to be doubted. If they were written to
Branwell, they might well make necessary a new biography of the Brontës. If they were written to Charlotte,
it is unlikely that they will reveal anything ; if to Anne,
though Emily seems to have loved her, they will be as
discreet as though they were addressed to a child.

It is an instance of Shorter's obtuseness in all things
relating to Emily Brontë that he should have written :
" It is certain that her own letters to her sisters, and
particularly to Anne, must have been peculiarly tender,
and in no way lacking in abundant self-revelation ". If
by " abundant self-revelation ", Shorter meant no more

* "The Brontës and their Circle ", by Clement K. Shorter.

than chatter about dogs and birds, or domestic details
that he might have hastened to publish in a domestic
journal, he may have been justified. Emily had two
lives. Her superficial life, the life of the daughter at the
parsonage, which she is commonly praised for having led
with dutiful heroism, was not in her eyes heroic. It was
the activity in the midst of which she had learned how
to feed upon the spirit within her. Those biographers
who insist that she sickened and came near to death when
separated from her moors have, I think, missed the root
of her desire for Haworth. That the bleak countryside
was friendly to her is true, but can scarcely have been
all the truth of a hunger so imperative. She clung to
her duties at the parsonage as visionary and contempla-
tive men cling always to the discipline that they have
cultivated as an enablement of their vision. The vision
was her secret, but of the unconcealed life that was its
condition she could write with a pleasing candour.
Never did feminine genius whine less against household
drudgery, for the good reason that her acceptance of it
was complete and her spirit too powerful to admit it as
an impediment.

I am quite contented for myself : not as idle as formerly,
altogether as hearty, and having learnt to make the most
of the present and long for the future with the fidgetiness
that I cannot do all I wish ; seldom or never troubled with
nothing to do, and merely desiring that everybody could be
as comfortable as myself and as undesponding, and then we
should have a very tolerable world of it. . . . Anne and I
should have picked black-currants if it had been fine and
sunshiny. I must hurry off now to my turning and ironing.*

For one who remembers of what other writing she
was capable, there is reason enough here for loving her.
Thus she may have written to her sisters, and her letters
would enable us to see her at work in the kitchen at

* " The Brontës and their Circle."

Haworth, and to love her as much for her reticences as for what she told. But such letters would not abundantly reveal her self, for Emily's self was set apart from all these things and was profoundly secret. She communicated it in her art because, being an artist who drew from the distillations of her spirit, and not, as Charlotte did, from external and observed sources, she could not do otherwise, but she was reluctant that her art should confess her to the world. She was angry when Charlotte dragged out her poems. She played for years the Gondal game with Anne, because to write poems and histories about an imaginary people gave her, even at her own fireside, a saving anonymity of form. " Emily," says Anne, " is writing the Emperor Julius's life. She has read some of it, and I want very much to hear the rest. She is writing some poetry, too. I wonder what it is about ? " It was probably about one of three things — the complete mystical experience that Emily appears to have enjoyed at some time in her early youth ; her abiding desire, which made all other desires relatively unimportant to her, for repetition of it ; or a partial re-experience — one of many, as I interpret her — from which, in an agony of spiritual disappointment, she had been dragged back.

When her critics have wearied of calling her "pagan ", which she was not, some have spoken of her as a mystical poet without fully appreciating how much truth is contained in their own words. Miss May Sinclair *— though an under-estimate of Branwell led her to dangerous conclusions and a strangely irrelevant twinge of feminism darkened her counsel now and then — was fully aware that Emily is of the company of Blake, not indeed in manner nor in faith, but in her capacity for spiritual absolutism. Miss Sinclair spoke of her as having been " in love with the Absolute ", and we need seek no

* " The Three Brontës ", by May Sinclair, 1912.

phrase more apt. She added that Emily " was a mystic, not by religious vocation, but by temperament and by ultimate vision ", and that none can comprehend her genius who does not himself, with " passion and sincerity ", embrace the idea of " the illusory nature of time and of material happenings ". This could not have been better said. But neither Miss Sinclair nor Madame Duclaux, whose early biography * has proudly endured long critical tests, seems to have realized how concrete, how definite, how specialized, Emily Brontë's spiritual adventure may have been.

Here we are on dangerous ground — dangerous because no theory about Emily Brontë's inner life is capable of final proof, doubly dangerous because, in many minds, the Brontës are an obsession which, while it lasts, attaches to them the privileges and penalties of Caesar's wife. We know that they were passionate writers, and that Emily was the most passionate. We know, or should know if we have remarked elsewhere the fruits of imaginative genius, that to infer from this alone that Charlotte was in love with Héger or that Emily experienced the satisfactions or even the desires of the flesh is unwarrantable. But Miss Sinclair, writing in 1911, went too far. She was violently scornful of those who then accepted the possibility of Charlotte's having been in love with Héger, she regarded the suspicion as an attempt to belittle the genius of a woman novelist ; she said that Charlotte, being " pure, utterly pure from all the illusions and subtleties and corruptions of the sentimentalist ", was incapable of " feeling in herself the possibility of passion " ; and, following Mrs. Gaskell, the only source then available, she quoted a fragment of one of Charlotte's letters to Héger in support of the conception of her heroine as a " fiery-hearted Vestal ". Two years later this letter and three others were published in full in *The Times* (July 29th,

* " Emily Brontë ", by Mary F. Robinson (Madame Duclaux), 1883.

1913). It was seen that Mrs. Gaskell, who may have been shown the originals by Héger, as Mr. Benson * supposed, but who more probably worked from a copy or copies retained by Charlotte, had been discreetly selective. That Charlotte loved Héger was established. The indignant rhetoric of Miss Sinclair was seen to have been thrown away, for the artist's repute was not touched.

The incident would not be worth its place here if it were not that rhetoric of the same colour has been, and is still being, used in defence of Emily's absolute chastity of act and wish, and that the publication of new material might at any moment cause this rhetoric to perish. Someone may dare to say that Emily, too, was in love. "But we shall at least know that he has made it up", said Miss Sinclair. "And even so, it will have been better for that man if he had never been born. He will have done his best to destroy or to deface the loveliness of a figure unique in literature." What an obsession is this! Who would feel that anything essential in the woman was defaced if it were proved that she had loved a man, or whose adoration of her genius be lessened? It is true that fiery genius is extremely rare in women who lack sexual impulse, and there may exist, in some minds, a wish to preserve so great a rarity, but this is not a good reason for saying, with Miss Sinclair, that " when Emily wrote of passion, she wrote of a thing that, as far as she personally was concerned, not only was not and had not been, but could never be ". There is none but speculative evidence for this sweeping statement. There is at present none but speculative evidence against it. In each reader's knowledge of women and in his biographical interpretation of the works, the subject may be allowed to rest until new evidence is forthcoming.

Let us, then, examine the works without seeking to prove in them either that Emily was in love with her

* " Charlotte Brontë ", by E. F. Benson, 1932.

brother or with any other man, or that she was incapable of bodily desire. It is unnecessary to proceed to either of these extremes, for the poems do not require it, and, though the closeness of Emily's later association with Branwell is deeply relevant to the authorship of " Wuthering Heights ", there is no just cause for assuming or suspecting that her love for him, if she loved him, was abnormal, except in the sense in which all emotional states were, by intensification and a disease of secrecy, made abnormal within the walls of Haworth. It is true that Charlotte's behaviour to Branwell, her envenomed exclusion of him from her life during the period in which " Wuthering Heights " was being written, is not fully accounted for either by his pleasures of the inn or by the suggestion that, having been herself denied in her passion, she was made morally indignant and resentful by her brother's disgrace at Thorp Green. Charlotte had many faults, but she was not a petty, spiteful spinster : there must have been better reasons than these for the long continuance of her hatred. It is true, also, that she displayed an extraordinary eagerness to obliterate all traces of her sister's private life, and that there is a hint of baffled terror in her reticences when she writes of Emily. On these and other indications it might be possible to build up a theory that the relationship of Branwell and Emily was one that displeased Charlotte, and that she wished to conceal the nature of it. But the evidence is all conjectural, and reacts against itself. We shall be wise to put this theory out of mind, and to proceed, for lack of available proof, on the assumption that it is altogether unfounded.

It remains as fact that Emily wrote poems of love, that many lines in those poems have the quality of supreme genius, and that supreme genius does not appear in love-poems written by those who are without experience or love. This argument has been a stumbling-block to those who are determined to disallow in Emily the love of man, but it need not have been so. They have gone to fantastic lengths in an endeavour to avoid a logic which seemed to them to be destructive of their theory. They have divided the poetry into Gondal verses and personal verses, being careful always to classify the love poems as Gondals — that is, as poems expressing the passion, not of Emily herself, but of one fictitious character in the Gondal cycle for another.

To this argument there are two replies : the first, that many of the Gondal ascriptions are extremely doubtful ; the second, that even where a poem is Gondal beyond dispute, it is often personal also beyond reasonable dispute, the Gondal form being no more than a cloak for personal feeling, or perhaps even a liberation of it. Clear proofs that Emily so used the Gondal form are to be found in two familiar poems, " The Prisoner " and " Remembrance ". The opening of " The Prisoner ", telling how narrator and gaoler visit a dungeon and speak with a female prisoner confined there, is evidently fictitious, probably Gondal, and, like all Emily's work, when written deliberately and not dictated by the spirit within her, second-rate :

About her lips there played a smile of scorn :
" My friend," she gently said, " you have not heard me mourn ;
When you my kindred's lives, *my* lost life, can restore,
Then may I weep and sue, — and never, friend, before ! " *

No genius was needed for the composition of that ; but suddenly, with so violent a flash that I am inclined to wonder whether the connexion between the earlier and the later sections of the poem is not an editorial error, Emily Brontë speaks :

" Still, let my tyrants know . . ." †

* " The Complete Poems of Emily Jane Brontë ", edited by Clement Shorter, arranged and collated, etc., by C. W. Hatfield (1923), p. 15.

† Shorter and Hatfield, p. 7.

The superb stanzas, the clearest, the most persuasive description of mystical experience in our language, are so familiar that they need not be quoted here. They are enough to undermine the theory that those poems which have a fictitious form are necessarily impersonal. An examination of " Remembrance " completes the destruction of that theory. Whose death is lamented in these verses we do not know — not Branwell's for it was written not later than March 1845.

> Cold in the earth — and the deep snow piled above thee,
>   Far, far removed, cold in the dreary grave !
> Have I forgot, my only Love, to love thee,
>   Severed at last by Time's all-severing wave.*

If words have meaning — above all, if the music of poetry has a significance distinct from that of its words — this is a lament written by one experiencing a personal emotion. We must not be over-precise in our interpretations. The poem is unquestionably Gondal in form, one of the two MSS. in which it exists being headed, " R. Alcons to J. Brenzaida ". The external circumstances may well have been dictated by the necessities of the Gondal fiction, and we should be rash to assume that the creature lamented in Emily's own heart had been dead while " fifteen wild Decembers, From those brown hills [had] melted into spring ". Nor is it necessarily to be believed that when she cried,

> Sweet Love of youth, forgive, if I forget thee,

she was providing commentators with evidence of an early passion. It is by no means impossible that the personal thought within the Gondal form was directed to her dead sister. But speculation on this identity is unfruitful. It is enough that the poem, together with " The Prisoner ", be accepted as disproof of the theory that verses with a Gondal form are to be regarded as impersonal.

* Shorter and Hatfield, p. 7.

Thus the whole body of poems is released to equal criticism, and we may range them, side by side with " Wuthering Heights ", as the basis of our interpretation of the author. I would add here, in parenthesis, that I accept Emily as substantially the author of " Wuthering Heights " without believing for a moment that Branwell was physically incapable of collaborating with her, or that he lacked qualities of imagination and experience that would have given value to his collaboration. The evidences that he had some share in the work are numerous and independent ; Mr. E. F. Benson has so ably martialled them in his life of Charlotte that they need not be reviewed. Miss Alice Law* takes in Branwell's defence an extremer position, into which it is hard to follow her, but her research has done much to make it seem probable that the brother contributed to the sister's work. What was the extent of that contribution we cannot know. Mr. Benson would " assign the first two chapters, pompous and monstrous in style, with their Lockwood motif which once announced is heard no more ", to Branwell, and, though the admitted structural flaw in the opening does not persuade me, in a book of such confused architecture, that two hands have been at work, it does seem to be true that the two opening chapters are burdened with a facetiousness from which the rest of the book is exempt.

What gives to Emily her unique place among English novelists is that her imagination, when in full cry, was unembarrassed by the curse of " humour ", which, when found in a tragic writer, is often equivalent to destructive self-consciousness. " Wuthering Heights ", said a contemporary reviewer † in one of the cuttings preserved by Emily in her desk,

* " Patrick Branwell Brontë ", and " Emily Jane Brontë and the Authorship of ' Wuthering Heights ' ", both by Alice Law.

† Quoted in " Emily Brontë ", by Charles Simpson, 1929, pp. 174-5.

is a strange, inartistic story. . . . "Jane Eyre" is a book which affects the reader to tears ; it touches the most hidden sources of emotion. "Wuthering Heights" casts a gloom over the mind not easily to be dispelled.

. . . The book sadly wants relief. A few glimpses of sunshine would have increased the reality of the picture and given strength rather than weakness to the whole. There is not in the entire dramatis personae a single character which is not utterly hateful or thoroughly contemptible.

This, as Charlotte indicated in her preface, is untrue ; the reviewer who wrote it was a fool. But when he pleaded for "a few glimpses of sunshine" he was representative of a school of criticism that persists to our own day. "Wuthering Heights" is great, not for its story, which is rash and confused ; not for its drawing of recognizable or virtuous character, though, as Charlotte said, Nelly Dean has "true benevolence and homely fidelity" and Edgar Linton is "an example of constancy and tenderness" ; but for its power to communicate a vision and, in communicating it, to concede nothing to those who clamoured then — and clamour still when they cannot endure the ecstatic fire, the "horror of great darkness" — for "relief", for "glimpses of sunshine", for "increased reality". And it is not to be denied that the hand which wrote the first two chapters was capable of these concessions. It was not cheerful, but it had a funereal, polysyllabic facetiousness strikingly contrasted with the lightning of Emily at her best.

"The Lord help us !" he soliloquized in an undertone of peevish displeasure, while relieving me of my horse ; looking, meantime, in my face so sourly that I charitably conjectured he must have need of divine aid to digest his dinner, and his pious ejaculation had no reference to my expected advent.

This could scarcely be worse : Branwell may have written it. But if we harshly attribute it to him, we are in danger of repeating the error common in Shakespearian scholars who will not permit their Homer to nod. Emily may well have been guilty, if she was writing self-consciously before the genius within her had possessed her pen.

That Branwell had a hand — or, if not a hand, a contributory mind — in the book is sufficiently established by evidence external to the text. That Emily was the substantial author is, nevertheless, beyond doubt. Charlotte, we know, could lie in a good cause, particularly when the secrets of authorship were at stake; but all her letters about Ellis Bell go to prove that she believed "Wuthering Heights" to have been written by Emily. This — the contacts of Haworth being what they were — is itself strong evidence for Emily's authorship. Nor is there any reasonable motive to account for prolonged deception by Emily, or for Branwell's having permitted her, if the book was not hers, to rob him of his author's vanity. It has been said by one theorist * that Charlotte wrote it — a suggestion manifestly ridiculous; as well attempt to prove that Sir Walter Scott wrote "Kubla Khan".

Emily's genius is plainly dominant in "Wuthering Heights", unless we are to assume that the manuscripts of the poems are fraudulent; for whoever wrote the poems wrote "Wuthering Heights", the same unreality of this world, the same greater reality of another, being in them both. The poems and the novels are twins of a unique imagination. They have the same prosaic lapses, the same poetic transcendence; they have the same obsession with the idea of imprisonment and of supernatural visitants; the same swift alternation between two seemingly contradictory ideas of death.

One instance of this from the novel must suffice. In Chapter XV Heathcliff visits Catherine, who is dying and big with child.

* "The Key to the Brontë Works. The Key to Charlotte Brontë's 'Wuthering Heights', etc.", by John Malham Dembleby, 1911.

Heathcliff had knelt on one knee to embrace her ; he attempted to rise, but she seized his hair, and kept him down. . . . " Don't torture me till I am as mad as yourself," cried he, wrenching his head free, and grinding his teeth. The two, to a cool spectator, made a strange and fearful picture. Well might Catherine deem that heaven would be a land of exile to her, unless with her mortal body she cast away her mortal character also.

But later Catherine says :

" Oh, you see, Nelly, he would not relent a moment to keep me out of the grave. *That* is how I'm loved ! Well, never mind. That is not *my* Heathcliff. I shall love mine yet ; and take him with me : he's in my soul. And," she added, musingly, " the thing that irks me most is this shattered prison, after all. I'm tired of being enclosed here. I'm wearying to escape into that glorious world, and to be always there : not seeing it dimly through tears, and yearning for it through the walls of an aching heart ; but really with it, and in it. . . . I shall be incomparably beyond and above you all. I *wonder* he won't be near me ! " She went on to herself. " I thought he wished it. Heathcliff, dear ! you should not be sullen now. Do come to me, Heathcliff."

The contrast between these two passages is not to be mistaken. It is the contrast between the two planes on which Emily Brontë conducted her life — the plane on which Ellen Nussey and Charlotte observed her and the plane that was the basis of her mystical poetry. On the first, she deemed " that heaven would be a land of exile to her ". When death approached, she struggled against it. " I have seen nothing like it," wrote Charlotte, " but indeed, I have never seen her parallel in anything. Stronger than a man, simpler than a child, her nature stood alone." She was not, as her own diary proves, discontented ; she was reconciled with life, and could, in her own solitary way, be happy ; to which Ellen Nussey bore testimony, confirming Charlotte. " On the top of the moor or in a deep glen, Emily was a child in spirit for glee and enjoyment ; or when thrown entirely on her own resources, she could be vivacious in conversation and enjoy giving pleasure." And Miss Nussey supplies the link between the two aspects of this girl whose " extreme reserve was impenetrable ". Few people, she said, " have the gift of looking and smiling as she could look and smile. One of her rare expressive looks was something to remember through life." These looks were all that Emily revealed of that other plane, experience of which made her feel that on earth she was a prisoner. She was tired of being enclosed. She was weary to escape to " that glorious world " of which, I believe, she had once enjoyed immediate apprehension. All her life, all her poems, all those parts of " Wuthering Heights " that bear the stamp of vision were dedicated to her desire that this direct experience might be repeated, that she might be again " really with it, and in it — not seeing it dimly through tears, and yearning for it through the walls of an aching heart."

There are in the poems indications enough that this experience, this achievement of the Absolute with which she was ever afterwards " in love ", was identified in her mind with an individuality, known to be ghostly in its relation to the earthly plane, but having for her an unforgettable reality and possibly an anthropomorphic form. If this be true, there is no need for the curious to ask with which of her father's curates Emily was in love, nor for the too eager advocates of a sexless soul to explain away her passion as Gondal. Nor, in recognizing this truth, need we give to it the harsh outline of Romer Wilson's Demon Lover.* Emily Brontë may, or may not, have loved in the flesh ; certainly no love poems have ever been more free than hers of erotic imagery ; but, however this may be, the key to her art, with which alone we are deeply concerned, lies, not in a bodily passion,

* " All Alone ", by Romer Wilson.

but in a spiritual ecstasy having, for her, the form of possession at once blissful and terrible. This idea is continually expressed in her poems :

> What I love shall come like visitant of air,
> Safe in secret power from lurking human snare ;
> Who loves me, no word of mine shall e'er betray,
> Though for faith unstained my life must forfeit pay.*

From the possession of night when—

> Thought followed thought, star followed star
> Through boundless regions on ;
> While one sweet influence, near and far,
> Thrilled through, and proved us one ! — †

she awoke to the agony of daybreak and consciousness of the earthly plane. The sun rose ; she hid herself in her pillow.

> It would not do — the pillow glowed,
> And glowed both roof and floor ;
> And birds sang loudly in the wood,
> And fresh winds shook the door. ‡

In October 1845, having described the spirit that " sent his dazzling gaze down through that ocean's gloomy night ", she told how she had sought continually and in vain for him :

> I've watched and sought my lifetime long ;
> Sought him in heaven, hell, earth, and air,
> An endless search, and always wrong. §

And often, I think, when she seems to be lamenting the death of a human being, and thrusting from her mind the too powerful memory of the " sweet Love " of her youth, the power of this spirit to elude her is the force behind her words :

---

* Shorter and Hatfield, p. 53. † *Ibid.* p. 3.
‡ *Ibid.* p. 4. § *Ibid.* p. 6.

Then did I check the tears of useless passion —
    Weaned my young soul from yearning after thine ;
Sternly denied its burning wish to hasten
    Down to that tomb already more than mine.

And, even yet, I dare not let it languish,
    Dare not indulge in memory's rapturous pain ;
Once drinking deep of that divinest anguish,
    How could I seek the empty world again ? *

Seven years earlier (November 3rd, 1838), she was already telling of the same loss :

    O Dream ! where art thou now ?
      Long years have passed away,
    Since last from off thy angel-brow
      I saw the light decay.†

On May 25th of the same year her statement, within the Gondal form of " Gleneden's Dream ", is direct and unmistakable :

    Watcher, in this lonely prison,
      Shut from joy and kindly air,
    Heaven, descending in a vision,
      Taught my soul to do and bear.‡

But she cannot deny herself her ecstatic voyages, though their incompleteness is torment to her.

Oh ! dreadful is the check — intense the agony —
When the ear begins to hear, and the eye begins to see ;
When the pulse begins to throb, the brain to think again ;
The soul to feel the flesh, and the flesh to feel the chain.
Yet I would lose no sting, would wish no torture less. . . . §

Sometimes the vision approached her by day :

    Methought, the very breath I breathed
      Was full of sparks divine,
    And all my heather-couch was wreathed
      By that celestial shine ! ‖

---

* Shorter and Hatfield, p. 8.   † *Ibid.* p. 97.
‡ *Ibid.* p. 85.   § *Ibid.* p. 16.   ‖ *Ibid.* p. 19.

Sometimes by night she longed for it :

> Yes, Fancy, come, my Fairy Love !
>   These throbbing temples softly kiss ;
> And bend my lonely couch above,
>   And bring me rest, and bring me bliss.*

Page after page of her poems proclaims the same hunger for an experience, having the force of absolute possession, once known, still tasted, but now, in its finality, denied to her.

Burn then, little lamp ; glimmer straight and clear —
Hush ! a rustling wing stirs, methinks, the air :
He for whom I wait thus ever comes to me ;
Strange Power ! I trust thy might ; trust thou my constancy. †

To one who had known this reality, all other failure was less than her failure to recapture it, and over such a one the world had no power. Death appeared to her, in one aspect, as an end of the blissful torture she would not have lessened ; in another aspect, as a possible reversal of her failures — an opportunity to be " really with and in " the supreme familiar spirit. She did not know whether to dread death as a cessation or to desire it as an opportunity. She did not know whence her familiar spirit came, from Heaven or from Hell ; she did not know whether, in the Christian view, her blisses were evil or good ; she was not certain that, in going from this world, she might take her ecstasy with her. " I shall love (*my* Heathcliff) yet ; and take him with me : he is in my soul," said Catherine, and though it would be foolish to suggest that Heathcliff was no more than an embodiment of Emily's vision, seen in its aspect of evil, it is unquestionably true that he often, while she wrote the novel, so appeared to her, and that Catherine's passion for a man was, in this sense, an expression of Emily's passion for her absolute visitant. " ' Heathcliff,

* Shorter and Hatfield, p. 21.   † *Ibid.* p. 53.

dear ! you should not be sullen now. Do come to me, Heathcliff.' "

Novel and poems are one. Both, in the intervals when genius slackened and talent was needed to fill the gap, weakened, for Emily had not a tutored talent, consistently at her service. She could write verses as trivial as Anne's ; she could compose a strange "inartistic story". But she had an extraordinary power, when the secret virtue commanded her stresses and her open vowels, to change a commonplace metre into a winged charge of the squadrons of the spirit, and, because she was delivered from humour and could permit a woman, vehement with a lover, to retain "in her closed fingers a portion of the locks she had been grasping " ; because she wrote, when she wrote well, on the plane of her own vision, without embarrassment, without fear, she has left behind her a novel that cannot perish. That cannot perish, not because it is faultless, but because it has already transcended its faults. Its appeal is not to reason, but to perception ; it is not an argument, but a spell. Like the poems, it is not a criticism of this life, but the evocation of another, and, like its author, it is not to be compared. "The worst of it is ", wrote Charlotte to Mr. Williams, having tried laboriously to explain Heathcliff by his unfortunate upbringing ; " the worst of it is, some of his spirit seems breathed through the whole narrative in which he figures : it haunts every moor and glen, and beckons in every fir-tree of the Heights." This is the book's miraculous unity. It is possessed by Heathcliff, who was " in " Emily's soul.

The
Uncommon Man

NONE of the tasks of a historian is more difficult than that of distinguishing a man from his acts. Bonaparte was not only a general and a legislator ; he did not consist in his military and civil policy ; he was that unique animal, Napoleon, son of Letizia, husband of Joséphine, prisoner of St. Helena, a child who became a boy, a boy who became a man, carrying within him always a sense of his continuous identity, aware, as we all are, that his acts were mysteriously independent of him and that whoever judged him by them was, to a great extent, basing judgment on an irrelevance. A man lives and has his being so largely in a realm of imagination that what are ordinarily called the facts of his life, even when they include his letters and his conversation, are extremely incomplete evidence of his nature. His thought between sleeping and waking, his small follies of hope and disappointment, his ideas of himself, a thousand secrets to which even he has not the key, are necessary parts of the whole truth, and all his works give the historian access to no more than a fragment of these fragments.

If this is the handicap of historians, how much greater is our own in forming an estimate of our contemporaries ! In considering our personal acquaintance we have, it is true, one great advantage — the advantage of hearing, seeing, touching — for the rising colour of a cheek, the touch of a hand, the turn of a head, may give more of the truth's essence than all the Confessions of Rousseau. But how dare we generalize about our contemporaries whom we have not seen, touched, or heard ? How shall we venture to judge them by their acts or their recorded behaviour ? Yet to do so is one of those terrible approximations to which all of us — and statesmen above all — are compelled. The King's Government must be carried on. To rule, to legislate, is to generalize. Even sociologists, economists and statisticians have, therefore, a reason for their existence ; and the rest of us, since we must have a language in which to discuss the affairs of mankind, may be driven now and then into saying : " The people need . . ." or " Women are . . ." Whatever sentence begins with such words is, we know, inevitably a lie. But how are they and their like to be altogether avoided ?

Perhaps they cannot be, but the confusion of thought which arises from them may be lessened if we resolve to treat them all with profound suspicion — avoiding them wherever possible, understanding that, even when used cautiously, they cannot be more than the roughest of approximations, and, finally, correcting their tendency to error by applying to them the imagination with which we check any sweeping statement about our own friends. To apply this corrective unflinchingly is to-day required of men unwilling to be dupes. The vast, deceptive generalizations are being proclaimed with alarming naïveté. Sociology, which no genuine student of the subject has ever claimed to be an exact science, is being treated by pious amateurs as if it were. The capital letters with which " The People " and " Women " and " The New World " are spelt grow daily in stature and decline in discrimination. A creature called the Common Man has been raised up, and the Coming Age is said to be his. In certain contexts, the phrase is a legitimate convenience and is no more to be intolerantly ruled out than other phrases in the same kind ; but let us beware of supposing that a gift of revelation is inherent in the use of it. At its best, it is neither newer nor more profound nor more precise than " the Man-in-the-Street ".

If " Women are . . ." is, in most cases, a rash generalization with more of lying than of truth in it, " The Common Man is . . ." has even less title to the round-eyed faith of the world.

I believe that the coming age will be that of the Uncommon rather than of the Common Man, and have two reasons for believing this : first, that the concept of the Common Man is as false, inhuman and fictitious as the once prevalent notion of the Innocent Savage ; second, that my experience of men and women has taught me that they love their differences, their separate identities, and will not tolerate the sea-green regimenters who, in the name of social equality, seek to impose upon them a grey sameness of the soul. The regimenters will reply that a novelist whose novels are not political, and who, it is therefore to be presumed, has always inhabited an ivory tower of privilege, is disabled from opinion on this matter by his ignorance of " the masses ". The supreme insolence of the regimenters, and their most profound delusion, is their belief that " the masses " exist. There is no ivory tower so windowless as theirs. Whoever has had genuine experience of life outside a social-betterment committee or a statistical bureau and has worked with the so-called masses instead of grinding a political axe on their backs ; whoever has kept watch on a bridge or served in an engine-room or gone away with a boat's crew or fought in trenches or made long marches or been a prisoner for long months in close company or been sunk in the North Sea, or has been or done or suffered all these things — whoever, that is to say, has learned his fellow-creatures outside the sheep-pens of the social dogmatists knows that each one of them is an uncommon man and is incapable of thinking of himself or of the man next him in any other terms. A ship's company is not a herd — nor, for that matter, except to our ignorance of animals, is a herd itself !

Woe betide the priest who looks for the Common Parishioner and not for the child of God, or the captain who is not a distinguisher of sailors, or the midshipman whose cutter's crew is for him an Average multiplied by twelve ! The boat is called away at night. The shore is distant by a long spell under oars. The dip of the blades, the click-clock of the crutches, the steady body-swing, the dim monotony of twelve faces half hidden, half revealed : might not the midshipman on his dickey almost be lulled into supposing himself confronted by a dozen specimens of the Common Man ? Not when shore is reached and the boat waits, tied up to a wall, and pipes are lighted. Then each man is distinct ; alone in his case of flesh as all spirits are, as Nelson was ; with a sense of association, never of sameness, and, ultimately, incommunicable. Look in the twelve faces : the Common Man is not there, nor any awareness of him.

This is not a mean age of compromise and cowardice and the shelving of responsibility upon a phrase. It is true that the conditions of modern war, rightly called " total ", appear to press all but a very few down into the common rut, harnessing men to machines, paring away by each restriction upon living the area of taste, dissolving private judgment (or seeming to dissolve it) in the acceptance of discipline. " Seeming " — but no more. Discipline does not dissolve private judgment any more than a rule of law dissolves it, but is rather an endorsement and proof of it in those who, for the avoidance of tyranny, agree as free men to be disciplined. Nevertheless the " seeming " and the appearances have been enough to mislead many into supposing that this is a docile nation, desiring to be, averaged, classified, docketed, ironed out, jealous of great men, resentful of character, the dull fodder of a bureaucracy. Those who count on this may be violently undeceived. For many years now the natural bureaucrats, the purists of the blue-print and the coupon, aided by two wars — for war is the apotheosis of their system — have struggled to persuade men to be slaves for their own good. They promise to continue in this endeavour. When they contemplate the end of this war, it is for a kind of civil totalitarianism that they look with brightly eager eyes. Everything is to be regulated. From birth to death, we are all, for the benefit of our common soul, to live in a state of continuous war, excepting only the sound of guns. What, they ask, are we fighting for ? It is not for a regulated millennium ? The answer is : No, for our lives. But that answer is not convenient to those who specialize in millennia. They need clients and have invented one ; he is called the Common Man. They forget that man was born to be loved or hated, to plough a field or write a poem, to win a battle or lose it, to take a risk, to make his soul ; he is not on this earth to be counted as though he were one of a million beads on the adding-machine of some gargantuan and idiot child. A statesman who grasps this and bases his policy upon it will not be without followers in the cutter's crew. The slogan " Tear up the forms ! " would be as silly as all slogans, but, used unscrupulously, might win an election.

It is not an essayist's business to legislate but to examine the values, and the changes in them, which lie, or should lie if they are rightly discerned, at the root of policy ; and if it be true, as it seems to be, that the philosophy of the Uncommon Man will express, more nearly than its alternative, the desire and purpose of those who will survive this war, it is necessary to examine it closely, to ask what it is and what it implies. Like all considerable movements of thought, it is, in part, a revolt against the doctrines and the experience immediately preceding it — a revolt, in this instance, against the greyness of being regimented ; and force is added to it by the suspicion, which has become an assurance, that those who like to exercise a detailed control over the lives of others have used two wars as an opportunity to exalt as a polity desirable in itself a regimentation that is a bleak necessity of war. The Uncommon Man, having consented to restriction for the purpose of saving his life, finds that restriction itself is being exalted as an ideal. That it cannot be instantly removed at the end of a war he is well aware ; he is no fool and will curb his impatience ; but he is aware also that behind the burden of officials which the two wars have imposed upon society is a theory of officialdom which would treat him as the Common Man, and this theory is abominable to him. If it persists as a theory of government he will break it.

The difference between his philosophy and the so-called philosophy of the Common Man rests upon his belief that his life is his own and that he himself is primarily responsible for it. The Constitution of the United States offers an interesting analogy. All powers are in the individual States except those which they themselves have conferred upon the Federal Government. Any attempted encroachment by the Federal Government on the States' residuary powers is fiercely contested. The Uncommon Man regards himself as being possessed of all powers in his own life which he has not conferred upon the State ; the theorists of the Common Man take the opposite view : that the community is the source of power and that what men do is to be done by its consent, even by its direction — that is to say, uniformly so far as the lamentable differences between men permit. For example, in a society of Common Men there is to be uniformity of dress. The idea raised its head in this war. A shortage of material and labour, which was a good reason for restricting the quantity of each that a citizen might consume, was made an excuse to prevent him from using his assigned quantity in accordance with his taste. Though he might be willing to surrender for a coat of his choice twice the number of coupons required for a coat of the standard design, and though he would thus have absorbed less material and less labour than his friend who ordered two standard coats, he was denied this saving liberty. He had to be uniform for the sake not of economy but of uniformity. The area of his independence was reduced and his neighbours gained nothing. Though this instance of dress may seem trivial, it serves to illustrate the purpose of the regimenters and its deep unpopularity — for this particular dress-regulation had to be abandoned in March 1944.

There are two kinds of law — law that requires and law that forbids. At no time can the law that requires be altogether eliminated ; it is necessary to require that births be registered, or taxes paid, or that, in certain circumstances, men shall be trained as soldiers ; and it is probable that the complexity of modern international life will demand that the area of this positive law be increased. At the same time the negative law that forbids may also be increased, but this does not necessarily mean that liberty will be ground to dust between the upper and the nether millstones ; for negative law — the law, for example, which forbids A to hold B a prisoner without trial — may be a law protective of freedom. One law may have two aspects. The law that now prevents a man from having more than his share of food and clothing is, in this aspect, negative and protects a general liberty, but when it requires him to wear a particular coat, it is, in that aspect, positive and at enmity with freedom. The distinguishing character of those who see men not as individuals but as the Common Man is that they prefer positive to negative law, they desire to use the power of the State not only to prevent a free man from injuring others, but steadily to increase the area of compulsion and so of uniformity. Their argument is that they would compel men to act for their own good ; this is the justification of all positive law — for example, of that which requires a child to submit to education ; and no one denies that it is sometimes necessary. To refuse all positive law would be to revert to an extreme policy of laissez-faire, and this is neither possible nor to be desired. But there is a real distinction of values between those who wish to preserve and those who, in pursuit of the theory of the Common Man, wish to overthrow that balance between positive and negative law upon which has hitherto rested our whole conception of a community at once orderly and free. The distinction is by no means for lawyers only. The question is not " By what means shall I be governed ? " but " To what end ? " Are the people, synthesized as the Common Man, to be regarded as the material of Government, or is Government to be regarded as a method, convenient to differing men, of safeguarding a defined area of common interest ? Perhaps the most profound division between the two schools of thought is on the question of opportunity. What is it ? How is it to be used ?

There is agreement that disabilities ought to be removed in so far as nature has not made them irremovable. To remove them is generally regarded as being, after the duty of self-preservation from external enemies, a first charge upon the resources of a community. Among these disabilities are destitution and the fear of destitution. Thus far there is no dispute. It is after this point that the ways of thought diverge. What are men, freed from destitution, to do with their freedom ? Is it their principal purpose to raise the Common Man a little further above the subsistence level ? And then a little further ? And then further still ? In brief, is the purpose of living an increasing measure of comfort, physical safety and regimented amenities ? Is this all ? Is " equal opportunity " to mean, when we have it, only a ticket for an increasingly prosperous soup-kitchen ? If this is what it means in terms of the body, what does it mean in terms of the mind ? If the governing idea is to be that of the Common Man and all things are to be shaped to his supposed needs, education must conform to his conformity, and educational authorities, with a dutiful eye on the Common Boy, must deny exceptional opportunity to exceptional boys. Finally, if the balance between the law that requires and the law that forbids were to be more weighed down on the side of positive requirement, it would not seem enough to forbid a book to be seditious or libellous ; censorship would become positive ; men would not only have bounds put to their liberty to write what they pleased, but would be told what, in the interest of the Common Man, they were to write. To write is to think ; to think is to believe or disbelieve. There are no boundaries to the area of greyness into which men will be led who are duped by the fallacy of the Common Man.

Italia
Irredenta

IT must always be accounted to Byron for grace, even by those queer English who are either shocked or frightened by him, that he loved two things so different and so un-Byronic as Dante and "The Vicar of Wakefield", and could speak very hotly of German interference in things Italian. Soon after his thirty-third birthday he was reading Schlegel, and took a hearty dislike to him. He had, Byron admitted, "a great power of words", but there was "nothing to be taken hold of". As long as what he wrote about was the North, he was tolerable, "but still he speaks of things *all over the world* with a kind of authority that a philosopher would disdain, and a man of common sense, feeling, and knowledge of his own ignorance would be ashamed of". How little, we say, reading Byron, do the Germans change ! Always they succeed in convincing themselves that they have a better claim to other peoples' lands and literature than the peoples themselves. Their scholars have never tired of explaining Shakespeare to the English, and here, if you please, was Schlegel reproving the Italians for their neglect of Dante !

Read Schlegel [Byron continues]. Of Dante he says, " that at no time has the greatest and most national of Italian poets ever been much the favourite of his countrymen ". 'Tis false ! There have been more editors and commentators (and imitators, ultimately) of Dante than of all their poets put together. *Not* a favourite ! Why, they talk Dante — write Dante — and think and dream Dante at this moment (1821) to an excess that would be ridiculous but that he deserves it.

Schlegel had been rash enough to say that Dante's chief defect was a want of gentle feelings, and Byron is at his throat for the heresy. It is true, he says, that there isn't much scope for gentleness in Hell — but who *but* Dante could have introduced any gentleness at all into Hell ? Is there any in Milton's ? " No — and Dante's Heaven is all love and glory and majesty." But by one in the morning Byron had discovered a redeeming virtue, even in Schlegel :

I have found out, however, where the German is right — it is about "The Vicar of Wakefield ". " Of all romances in miniature (and, perhaps, this is the best shape in which romance can appear) ' The Vicar of Wakefield ' is, I think, the most exquisite." He *thinks* ! — he might be sure. But it is very well for a Schlegel. I feel sleepy and may as well get me to bed.

That was on the night of January 29th. Next day his thoughts are all of Italian liberty. The new watchwords are given him. " Things are fast coming to a crisis — *ça ira* ! . . . Something must be up in Piedmont — all the letters and papers are stopped. . . . This state of things cannot last long. The ferment in men's minds at present cannot be conceived without seeing it."

How consoling it is to find, in reading such passages in Byron's journal, that, as between Germans and Italians, our sympathies lie precisely where his lay ! It is among the tests of our values that they should so continue. That the Government of Italy in recent years has deserved ill of Europe, that it attacked France when France was down, that it sent bombers against England when England was hardest pressed, that, in brief, it has been untrue to the history of the Risorgimento, is no reason that, in our thoughts of Italy, we should be untrue to ourselves or fail to recognize that between what Italy has done and what Germany has done is the distinction between a mistake that is being and will continue for some time to be paid for, and an enduring evil, a profound corruption, a canker in the very heart of the Germans. No Englishman, as he allows his thought to carry him into the future, imagines himself in continuing enmity with Italians or believes that he will be excluded, or will wish to exclude himself, from their country. His idea of Italy is steadfast. He blames her — for the manner of her intervention, for her behaviour to Greece, above all for the vile company she keeps ; he has no other course than to fight her until that behaviour is redeemed, that company repudiated ; but it is possible for her to close the bracket of her wrongdoing and to become Italy again in his eyes. The idea of Italy is clouded by follies and misdeeds, but the clouds will pass and the sun shine out again.*

With Germany no such thing can be. Ultimately, beyond the lifetime of any now living, there may emerge another Germany possible to love and honour, but a new idea of Germany will have to be born, nourished, proved, brought to maturity ; the old idea which led many English to have respect and even affection for her between Byron's time and our own is dead, or ought to be dead, in the imaginations of men. That it was not altogether dead during and even after the last war has been sufficiently proved by its power to lull England and America during the twenty years' armistice. Certainly there were many who were persuaded in the years following 1914 that if what was called " Prussian militarism " were overthrown there would arise from within Germany herself an effective liberal and pacific opinion not irreconcilable with the idea of Germany that so many Victorians brought home from their visits there ; but no such opinion made itself effective ; such liberalism as there was became the screen behind which new aggression was prepared ; and nowadays not even the most

* This essay was first published on June 5th, 1943.

optimistic can conceal from themselves that what was once called the liberal heart of Germany, never much more than a weak, fluttering thing, has been eaten out. Those who listen for it to beat again, when this war is done, would do better to keep their ear to the ground for the first drum-taps of a new aggression or the first whining attempt to evade the consequences of this. That this time the ruse to persuade the non-German world to put down its guard may be not a Weimar Republic but some form of government designed to flatter and reassure the sentiment of the United States, or, alternatively, to conform to the Russian model, matters nothing. The underlying idea of Germany — that of a " Herrenvolk " temporarily denied their slaves — will remain what it is and, in fact, has been since Sadowa.

But no one who has known the Italians since the coming of Fascism has felt that the inmost spirit of Italy has been corrupted by it. Rightly or wrongly, it was at the outset widely believed to be an alternative to anarchical disintegration ; it was not, like Nazism, a tool of men whose aim was European conquest. Though it became imperialistic — and the Italian treatment of their subject peoples has never been pretty — its imperialism was neither mentally diseased nor insatiable. But what above all else distinguished it from its German counterpart was that it did not make Italians intolerable political fanatics in their private lives. They dressed themselves up, they marched and shouted and drilled ; harmless little trades-men frowned and glared and folded their arms in imitation of Il Duce ; but they were capable also of being " off duty " and retained their ancient character : their gaiety ; their faculty, unequalled in all the world, of becoming children when in the company of children ; their delight in fine individual craftsmanship, whether it were the skill of goldsmiths or the making of good paper. And all the business that Fascism thrust upon them did not deprive them of that gift which is in itself a mark of civilization — the gift of doing nothing without being haunted by an earnest sense of wasting time.

A military procession in Milan or Florence was one thing, and very tiresome to the peace-loving, but to walk on the ancient ramparts of Lucca was another — there everyone was smiling and at ease, and the people who carried newspapers under their arms (but seldom read them) belonged to a civilization from which the ugly headlines were altogether remote. Few Italians have ever had any delusions about war. It is to them what it is to us — an evil sometimes inevitable ; then, man for man, they will fight bravely, as long as they have any kind of heart in it ; but to fight the English they are not accustomed, the Austrians were designed by a merciful Providence to be their antagonists, and to suffer for Germany's sake is no part of their scheme of things. If we try to see this war from the Italian point of view, the prospect is overwhelmingly black. However it falls out, it cannot be to their advantage. Only by losing the war, or by having the drastic courage to abandon it, has Italy a hope of freeing herself from the German incubus and becoming Italy again. That she should become Italy again is clearly a European and a civilized interest, not only because historically she holds so great a part of civilization in charge but because she is not and has never been an excluding nation ; she has in high degree the dual virtue of being able to receive with grace and to give without self-consciousness ; and in all her stones and rivers, her cities and her countryside, there is a spiritual hospitality, conforming to the nature of her people, in which may flourish the wisdom of other nations as well as her own. Though the inherent incapacity of the Germans to conduct amphibious war has made them disastrous allies in the Mediterranean, Italy is still by right of geography a Mediterranean Power, and so will remain unless she disintegrate. The question is whether her adherence to Germany is to be so prolonged as to make her disintegration an inevitable condition of Germany's defeat, or whether the unity of Italy, which was for so long an English as well as an Italian cause, is to be again what it was in its origin — an essential part of the structure of liberty in Europe.

How that question will be answered depends not upon us but upon the length of time that passes before a proud nation decides to cut its losses and so limit them. Meanwhile, it is among the pleasant reassurances of our times to observe how, even among the great masses of Englishmen who have never been to Italy and whose political judgment has certainly not been captured by her enchantments, a distinction between Italians and Germans is steadily preserved, and it is felt that, whereas war with Germany is indeed a war between people and people, between two irreconcilable ways of life, war with Italy is a political tragedy, an absurd accident that cuts across the histories of the two nations concerned. We can still laugh with the Italians. It is, even, a cause of complaint against their Government that they should so quickly after the Tunisian collapse have spoiled a good joke by promoting General Messe to the rank of Field-Marshal, and indeed the English sense of humour, which in this struggle has been ominously withdrawn from the Germans, has never ceased to give a tang to the Italian war. When it is reported that Italian propagandists have been urging their listeners to " hate " us, the English endure it smilingly as they endured the German Hymn nearly thirty years ago, but German outbursts in the same kind are no longer lightly passed off, for the Germans are past a joke ; they have been saying the same thing and behaving in the same way for too many generations. They have traded too long upon Beethoven and offered too many little bunches of flowers to gullible tourists whose homes they intend to ravish. Their gross, tramping feet have trod the good of all our lives into the mud of their ambition. Germany is the great bore of Europe and has to be kept under restraint. Italy is very far from being in the same category. She is still an enemy to whom our troops attach almost affectionate nicknames, but " Fritz " is out of date.

This is the surface of things. The reason lies much deeper. Public opinion, in the end, takes its colour from the opinion of the few, and those English who have known Italy well have combined through a long stretch of years to acknowledge their debt to her. Her sunshine, the pleasantness of life on her hills and shores, her wealth in evidences of the past, have unquestionably accounted for much ; they have again and again given release to the English spirit, filling the traveller with that sense of well-being, of there being after all, as Byron said when he was dying, " qualche cosa di caro nel mondo ", from which not lassitude but energy springs ; but Italy's secret has always been something more than the wonder of her history or the grace of her living. In the genius of other nations — the philosophic earnestness of Germany as she once was, the tempered intellectualism of France, our own great austerities and abounding humours — there seems often to be something middle-aged, the virtue being a virtue of maturity, so that even in the work of young poets, even in Shelley's, there is a kind of deliberate balance between impulse and wisdom. In art, vitality proceeds from stress, and this stress in the English genius, and the corresponding stresses in the French and the German, have been marvellously productive. To say, in any derogatory sense, that there is something middle-aged in our quality would be ridiculous, and yet the word has meaning as pointer to what in Italy is unique — the running together and fusing in her of old age and youth, of evening with morning. Midday — yes, if you please, the glory of noon — is left out. The generalization cannot be pressed, but there is in it a truth of *feeling*, of atmosphere, if not, strictly, of criticism.

What one feels always in Italy is an extraordinary and direct mingling of freshness with repose, as though all life were sunset and sunrise, winter and spring. . It is consistent with her history that this should be so ; in the nineteenth century a new youth was grafted upon her old age ; and yet the quality itself goes back far beyond the Risorgimento : it is in Dante as it is in Leopardi, it is in the landscape that Bellini gave as a background to his Agony in the Garden, and in the Italian skies and the Italian air. No sea is so old as the Italian sea on a still night. The melancholy of time is gathered in it, all passion spent ; it mirrors the decay of princes and the forgetting of love ; all vanity is consumed in it ; but in the morning how it sings for Botticelli, as if with Venus in that hour it had been created ! None but an Italian — unless by a supreme miracle of spiritual interpretation, wrung out of the past, it were the Milton of " Il Penseroso " and " L'Allegro " — none but an Italian could make articulate this particular stress of the Italian spirit, and an Englishman who feels it, so that to be denied Italy is to be denied one of the promptings of life, feels it always with wonder, and beneath its influence is emancipated from the oftentimes too rigid custom of his own mind. Men bring their ideas to Paris that there they may be tested and given currency, for Paris, though not the goldmine, is the mint of ideas ; but to Italy they take themselves, sometimes in expectation and hope, sometimes in the crippling and weariness of their minds, and are renewed in her ; for Italy is the country of rebirth as well as of the Renaissance. Even Germans have found virtue there, though it is typical that Julius Caesar should have been Mommsen's god and that poor Schlegel — to Byron's intense irritation — should have written about gondolas on the Arno. But the Germans, it must be remembered, are soldiers; though they build ships well and fight them gallantly, they have never understood about ships; and what profit Shelley had in sailing paper-boats their scholarship is wondering still.

Ivan
Turgenev

" THE longer I live, the more I value horses that are not restive." Those who cry out continually for what they call the " dynamic " and sometimes even the " stark " in life and literature will scorn this sentence as an exaltation of tame men and tame horses. They will, of course, recognize in it the cold, indifferent tones of the Turgenev whom they so much despise, for they think of him as having been very much a ladies' carriage-horse, comfortably stabled, discreetly reined — how different from, how inferior to, the fierce, defiant Dostoevski, or Tolstoy, whose importance, we have lately been told, largely consists in his having described, in a book called " War and Peace ", the scenes of Stalin's victories. The works of Tolstoy and Dostoevski are understood to have their place in every up-to-date library, but Turgenev is a " period piece ", a writer of prose-poems and of love-stories about aristocratic women — precisely the man whom the dynamists of the back-parlour would expect to write : " The longer I live, the more I value horses that are not restive ".

Nevertheless, it was Tolstoy himself who wrote it, and in praise of Turgenev. He was writing to Strakhov, Dostoevski's biographer :

I have read your book. . . . He is touching and interesting, but one cannot set on a pedestal for the instruction of posterity a man who was all struggle. From your book I have learnt for the first time the whole measure of his mind. Pressense's book I have also read, but all his learning is spoilt by a flaw. There are beautiful horses : but if a trotter, worth, say 1000 rubles, suddenly proves restive, then —

beautiful and strong as it is — it is worthless. The longer I
live, the more I value horses that are not restive. You say
that you are reconciled to Turgenev. And I have come to
love him very much ; and, curiously enough, just because
he is not restive but gets to his destination — not like a
trotter that will not take one to the journey's end and may
even land one in a ditch. But Pressense and Dostoevski are
both restive ; and so all the erudition of the one and the
wisdom and heart of the other run to waste. Turgenev will
outlive Dostoevski, and not for his artistic qualities but because
he is not restive. . . .

The whole passage, which, with so much else, we owe
to Aylmer Maude's "Life of Tolstoy", is worth studying
by anyone who wishes to understand the nature and
independence of Turgenev's genius.

For reasons not mysterious Turgenev has fallen into
disrepute or, what is worse, into neglect. Even the
recent fashion for all things Russian had produced scarcely
a whisper of his name until his play " A Month in the
Country " was revived at the St. James's Theatre. He
was too little restive, too unspectacular, too moderate
and patient in spirit, to make an easy text for the para-
graphists ; he was, in brief, without " publicity value ".
This has been true not in England only and not only
to-day. Turgenev has never come easily to the majority.
To value him, and to value him for the right reasons,
has always been evidence of a discerning, a cultivated,
above all an unbrutal, taste. " Every page of his writing,"
said Joseph Conrad, " bears its testimony to the fatal
absence of callousness in the man." In his own country
he was doubly attacked because, being an aristocrat, he
was critical of the autocracy, and, being of a liberal mind,
would not hate with the men of violence. " The serene
Turgenev," said Conrad, " is under a curse."

For only think ! Every gift has been heaped on his cradle :
absolute sanity and deepest sensibility, the clearest vision and

the quickest responsiveness . . . an unerring instinct for the significant, for the essential in the life of men and women, the clearest mind, the warmest heart, the largest sympathy. . . . There's enough there to ruin the prospects of any writer. For you know very well, my dear Edward, that if you had Antinous himself in a booth of the world's-fair, and killed yourself in protesting that his soul was as perfect as his body, you wouldn't get one per cent. of the crowd struggling next door for a sight of the Double-headed Nightingale or of some weak-kneed giant grinning through a horse-collar.

It is bitter writing — one wonders what provoked Conrad to it — and, like all bitter writing, it is partly untrue. The " crowd " does not always turn away from Antinous to the weak-kneed giant. It is one of the blessed paradoxes that, though the " crowd " may itself be blind or be blinded, its posterity ultimately is not ; but it is true, though Conrad said it with too sweeping a vehemence — it is true, and Turgenev is proof, that genius of which the pre-eminent qualities are sanity, generosity and balance will suffer long periods of neglect during which a more startling power — Tolstoy's, for example, or Dostoevski's — successfully plays the Double-headed Nightingale at his own game. " The convulsed terror-haunted Dostoevski ", writes Conrad, and " the serene Turgenev ". Dostoevski, heaven knows, had other merits, but the crowd will always pay its penny to witness a convulsion ; even Tolstoy went off to see a man guillotined. The serene Turgenev has to wait for attention, serenity, in whichever meaning the word is used, not being a virtue that beats the drum.

In which sense did Conrad use the word " serene "—not, I believe, to mean " calm " and, still less, " complacent ", but, rather, strictly, to mean clear, translucent, light-admitting, for calmness was what Turgenev longed for, not what he possessed, and translucence was the supreme virtue of his mind as it was of his story-telling. What gave translucence to his mind was, in large measure, that generosity, that instinct of compassion, which forbade him the rhetoric of judgment and which his enemies mistook for indifference. What gave it to his story-telling — as even we know who must read him in English or French — was his insistence on form, for form is not, as the heathen suppose, a decoration, a frosting of the glass through which meaning comes, but a purification of it. But it is dangerous to lay emphasis now on the formal aspect of Turgenev's talent, for the world is shy of " style ", or was shy of it until very lately. Form had come to be thought of as an artificiality, an embroidery, not as what it is — a means to truth ; and it is not long since it was fashionable to believe that a reader who plunged through the loose shingle of — shall we say ? — Theodore Dreiser's prose was by that resounding deed of masochism performing a duty to literature. Turgenev was suspect because he seemed to move easily and enchanted his companion ; earnest readers demanded a little suffering for their money ; and as long as art is considered as a medicine, and not as a wine with the sun and the earth in it, this attitude of a patient towards it is likely to prevail. Turgenev, we have been told, is too smooth, too graceful, too charming, too much like Chopin, like Corot ; how can such a man be sincere ? We must not praise his style lest the whole world, in its passion for stark sincerity, stampede for the grumbling shingle and scatter its pennies before the grinning giant. But is the world so foolish ? Are these its values still ? This essay would not be written except in the faith that they are changing. It is not required that the whole city hurry to its lending library to demand " Fathers and Children " or " A Sportsman's Sketches " ; but if one young man be found who, being by heaven's grace a writer, lays down the piece of " reportage " that has entangled him and takes up instead " Torrents of Spring " and is set free — why, then, there is better than printer's ink on this page and a new face in the mirror ! *

But there remains, of course, this question of sincerity. Towards the end of his life there arose a school of critics, or rather a dozen schools of critics, who solemnly denied it in Turgenev. In his Russia, political feeling ran high and there was a heavy censorship on the expression of it. Imaginative literature was almost the only outlet, and even that was perilous. Therefore an exceptional responsibility was felt to lie upon imaginative writers who could command an audience in Russia and in Europe. They could be counted on the fingers of a hand and Turgenev was one of them. He must plead a cause — *my* cause. Edward Garnett stated the case excellently well :

The Englishman who finds it strange that Turgenev's pictures of contemporary Russian life should have excited such angry heat and raised such clouds of acrimonious smoke may imagine the fate of a great writer in Ireland to-day [1917] who should go on his way serenely, holding the balance level between the Unionists, the Nationalists, the Sinn Féin, the people of Dublin and the people of Belfast. The more impartial were his pictures as art, the louder would rise the hubbub that his types were " exceptional ", that his insight was " limited ", that he did not understand either the politicians or the gentry or the peasants, that he had not fathomed all that was in each " movement ", that he was palming off on us heroes who had " no real existence ". And, in the sense that Turgenev's serene and beautiful art excludes

* A strange and sad coincidence has touched me as I correct this essay on February 25th, 1944. I have been reading this morning Stephen Haggard's " I'll Go to Bed at Noon " and am reminded that he met his death on February 25th, 1943. This essay was first published two days later.

Haggard was in his thirty-second year. There can have been no more brilliantly sensitive example of the younger generation, and it is a reassurance to learn, on the authority of Christopher Hassall, who writes of Haggard's library, that the works of Turgenev were by him " especially beloved ".

thousands of aspects that filled the newspapers and the minds of his contemporaries, his detractors have reason.

To that nothing need be added, but it is worth remarking that Edward Garnett — a beloved teacher, a master of criticism, a brave servant of literature against whom no word of mine shall ever be spoken — allowed at least the tail of his coat to be caught in the trap.

So anxious was he to prove Turgenev a child of Liberty and to acquit him of indifference that he stressed the political or social symbolism of his novels almost to breaking point. Turgenev himself described Elena, the heroine of " On the Eve ", as " a new type of Russian life ", but Garnett says that she " stands for the rise of Young Russia in the 'sixties " and that " in sketching the dawn of love in a young girl's soul Turgenev has managed faintly, but unmistakably, to make spring and flourish in our minds the ineradicable, though hidden, idea at the back of Slav thought — the unification of the Slav races ". This is not untrue, nor is it irrelevant, for nothing which indicates an artist's attitude to his subject is irrelevant to criticism, but it lays a dangerously strong emphasis on one aspect of the truth — and on what, in the long view of Turgenev's art, will seem a decreasingly important aspect of it.

A young man of to-day — Turgenev's posterity — who goes to " On the Eve " or " Torrents of Spring " to be made happy and wise, will not be, and ought not to be, greatly troubled for Turgenev's approach to the Nihilists or his distance from them. What matters in Elena after eighty-four years is what matters in all Elenas after eighty-four years — " the young girl's soul ". Nothing else is of enduring interest except her body and the art which created her. It was the knowledge that this is true of love-stories, and that no contemporary symbolism can make it less true, which led Tolstoy, as a moralist,

to repudiate novels. It is in the light of his extremely
difficult relationship with Tolstoy that the value of
Turgenev and his " sincerity " have in the end to be
judged, but a study of this relationship must await
another occasion. Meanwhile, taking Turgenev for what
he was and not for what Tolstoy would have liked him
to be, it may be of interest to notice a peculiarity in him
of much greater importance than all the ideas of Slav
unity by which he was ever visited.

Just after Easter, 1880, when he was sixty-two years
old, he went to stay with Tolstoy, and an expedition to
shoot woodcock was arranged in his honour. Aylmer
Maude tells the story :

In the dusk of the spring evening, the Countess stood
beside him awaiting the flight of the birds. While he was
getting his gun ready, she asked him : " Why have you not
written anything for so long ? " Turgenev glanced round and
in his touchingly frank way, with a guilty smile, said : " Are
we out of hearing ? Well, I will tell you. . . . Whenever I
have planned anything it has been when I have been shaken
by the fever of love ! Now that is over : I am old and can
no longer either love or write." To Tolstoy, also, Turgenev
spoke of the change that had come over him — him for whom
love-affairs had formed so large a part of the joy of life. " I
had an affair the other day," he said, " and, will you believe
it, I found it dull ! " " Ah," exclaimed Tolstoy, " if only I
were like that ! "

Compare with this a passage from " A Month in the
Country ", written many years earlier when the novelist
was still young. Beliayev, little more than a student, has
said that he has imagined requited love to be a great
happiness. Rakitin, a man of thirty, replies :

RAKITIN : God grant you long preserve such pleasant con-
victions ! It's my belief, Alexey Nikolaitch, that love of every
kind, happy as much as unhappy, is a real calamity if you
give yourself up to it completely. . . . Wait a bit ! You will

learn what burning hatred lies hidden under the most ardent
love ! You will think of me when you yearn for peace, for
the dullest, most commonplace peace, as a sick man yearns
for health, when you will envy any man who is free and
light-hearted.

In this fragment of dramatic dialogue and in the conversation with the Countess Tolstoy, the tension of motive
in Turgenev declares itself. A character is defined by its
lines of tension, is lighted and warmed by them ; without
tensions it is commonplace and dull ; but its substance
is in the areas of peace which those lines include. A
character which has no areas of peace but is, in Tolstoy's
phrase, " all struggle ", will produce art " spoilt by a
flaw ", and a character which has lost its warming and
light-giving tensions will not produce art at all. " I had
an affair the other day, and, will you believe it, I found
it dull ! " It was extremely simple. For Turgenev the
tensions were released, the light had gone out.

But during his youth and maturity his tensions were
of such a kind as held him always between an adoration
of women and a knowledge of the " real calamity " of
yielding to love completely. Passionate love, in his stories,
is much less a subject for analysis as it was to Stendhal,
or a primitive force to be overcome by renouncements as
it was to Tolstoy, than an all-embracing enchantment
which creates, in a man or woman, a new personality
superimposed upon the old — so that, as love is added
to love, personality is not cancelled out but multiplied,
and Natalya Petrovna, for example, loving Rakitin in
one way, her husband in another, and the young Beliayev
in a third, is shown to us, in this profoundly compassionate play, as a woman not damnable for her inconsistencies
but, as it were, illumined and deepened by her syn-
chronized experience. Put it how you will. Say that
the under-painting and the glazes together, and not
separately, make the picture. Say that Turgenev's vision

is that which Jesus taught : of innocence within guilt, of youth within age, of eternity in the instant — of those supreme identities of the spirit which forbid our condemnations. Of all novelists, none had this vision as Turgenev had it. Blake had it and, from another angle, Baudelaire. Indeed, it is Turgenev's link with the Symbolists. Sometimes, when he wrote of men, it failed him, but never in his writing of women. As well as their interpreter, he is their mediator. His method is neither to conceal evil nor excuse it, but to penetrate and so transcend it, never idealizing (in the sense of falsifying) the thing observed, but seeking always " l'idée ", the absolute, behind the particular, and allowing the particular — the folly, the aberration, even the cruelty — to be transfused by it.

> Comment, amour incorruptible,
> T'exprimer avec vérité ?
> Grain de musc qui gis, invisible,
> Au fond de mon éternité !

The lines of Baudelaire's " Hymne " might well have stood at the head of any love-story by Turgenev, and certainly as epigraph to " A Month in the Country ". There are immaturities and passages of theatrical convention in the play which prevent it from being flawless as " First Love " is flawless, but Natalya Petrovna is a portrait in which, if the part is played translucently, a spectator may see Turgenev's style epitomized.

Nausicaa
and the Pelicans

ONE has to be on one's guard. On the evening before
a day off, there is dangerous magic in the air. It
is easy to hope too much, to dream too much, to catch
at the balloon-strings of illusion. How many years have
passed since, to a schoolboy coming out of school, a whole
holiday — two nights and a day without the bang of
a desk or the smell of linoleum or the clash of crockery
and hand-bells — was an imperilled eternity, like a full
rain-drop on the stem of a brier ! Who would have
supposed that that particular rapture would come again,
that hungry passion to be given for a few hours to one's
own purposes and solitudes ?

Yet now from the routine of war — the mud of jargon,
the wilderness of alphabetical committees, the fog of procedure — springs the same breathless wonder of release !
At the beginning of a day off, all things are possible.
The gravel is diamonded, there are lyrics in the trees.
Across the Horse Guards, into St. James's Park, away,
away, homeward now — and there are the pelicans,
re-met each morning on the way to work, transmuted
by the afternoon light, for, whatever the clock may have
said, it is little after five by the sun. A group is watching
them from the water's edge. The slouching battledress,
the girls in uniform, the old witch with her basket, the
long-nosed dog stretched upon the grass like a dog in
porcelain, are held in a glittering and tranquil air, as
though Botticelli were watching spring move towards
summer and Stanley Spencer had taken the brush from
his hand.

A hundred yards later, at Birdcage Walk, the incon-

gruousness of that judgment appears. The meaning it
had for an instant when the long-nosed dog rose and
stretched himself and there was an arc of light on his
trembling back is gone. The association of ideas was
extravagant, the criticism too subjective. On such an
evening one must be on one's guard. And yet it is the
same association of ideas (for a group of maidens at the
seashore is a subject for either painter) which, that night,
brings down from the shelf, as the bedside book even of
a lamentable non-Greeker, the Odyssey, and opens it at
the building of the raft and half-closes it when Nausicaa
has gone to her father's house, leaving the maidens and
Odysseus to follow her. There is no story like that story
to give a traveller heart upon his way. "Have pity on
me, for, after many trials and sore, to thee first of all am
I come. . . ." And Nausicaa had pity on him. "Then
the sun set, and they came to the famous grove, the
sacred place of Athene ; so there the goodly Odysseus
sat him down," and prayed, "and Pallas Athene heard
him ; but she did not yet appear to him face to face,
for she had regard unto her father's brother, who furi-
ously raged against the god-like Odysseus, till he should
come to his own country." O Greeks and Frenchmen
and Americans, Englishmen also, who are exiles in the
body or in the spirit, remember how he came to his own
country, and told of his adventures, and of Nausicaa last
of all. "This was the last word of the tale, when sweet
sleep came speedily upon him . . . unknitting the cares
of his soul."

It is among the marvels of the Odyssey's story-telling
that, in it, the years are included in the days. When
Odysseus met Nausicaa (so early as the Sixth Book) his
journey was nearly over, for but two days later, "when
the star came up that is brightest of all", his vessel "in
full course ran ashore, half her keel's length high, so well
was she sped by the hands of the oarsmen·", and they

lifted him out, " all as he was in the sheet of linen and the bright rug ", and laid him, still asleep, on his own sand of Ithaca. During the intervening day, the many years and adventures appeared in his recollection and in the story he told to Alcinous, so that one receives from the whole epic, when all is done, the impression so often made by life itself — an impression far less of chronological sequence, a stretched tape of orderly events, than of an imperfect palimpsest of experience upon which what is old has not been erased to make room for what is new, but appears through it, the new and the old taking colour from each other, the child from the man, the man from the child, so that, in certain moods, we seem to carry in the cup of our hands a distillation of our total experience. Such, in the conditions of war, is often the effect of a day off : all life is in it, shining or mourning in those precious hours, and however immediate occupations are chosen — whether to be alone or to seek friends company, to read or write or walk in the air — the past looks through them ; the years are included in the day.

To choose even immediate occupations requires a new selectiveness — almost the selectiveness of the absurd man in the absurd problem who is asked to choose twelve books with which to be cast ashore on a desert island. In the past, leisure was not so scarce that one was pressed by the fear of wasting its opportunity. The library was, so to speak, full of books ; neglect one to-day, and still it might be read to-morrow ; there was no threat of a desert island, no urgency of final choice. Now, in the morning, it is necessary to choose, and not easy, for such days are so short and rare that what is neglected in them may be lost for ever — a friend, perhaps, long unvisited, or the love of music long unheard, or the power of continuous reading, or the spur of solitude, or the gift of idleness ; and, indeed, one may fall into foolish alarm at the prospect of these losses until one reflects that to

be greedy of a thing is to lose it. Let it go, it will return
in due season ; for solitude and the company of friends
are aspects of the same spiritual exercise, music and sunshine are instruments of the same visitation ; all things
are in all. Each man's draught of experience depends
upon the hand he dips in the universal stream, and upon
his steadiness, without spilling it, to carry the water to
his lips and taste it there. Therefore, though we are to
be selective, it must be with an unjealous selectiveness,
without grabbing, without fear. Because life is short,
shall we poison its years with terror of its end ? Because
a day is short, shall its hours be frayed with running to and
fro ? There is a transcendent leisure, overriding all the
deprivations of time.

That, we dare not question, is the wisdom of the thing
— but how hard to live by ! All is in all, the wise men
say, for to know and believe this is to be invulnerable,
incapable of loss ; but we are men and women, deeply
vulnerable still as children are, and when the cupboard
is to be open for only a few hours it is the devil to choose
among our toys. In any case, so many of the toys we
want are put away on the topmost shelf until the Germans
are tired of their game, and perversely we long for them.
For example, to be at Lord's, for there nothing changes.
A new stand or a new scoring-board arises now and then,
bowlers cease to bowl trial balls, red bat-handles go out
of fashion, but there is always the same freshness in the
forenoon, the same air of hot endurance between luncheon
and tea, and, after tea, the same intensification of sound
and silence, the lengthening of shadows, the deepening
of the green, and, it may be, suddenly an unreal tension
exquisitely heightened so that each withdrawal to the
pavilion is the death of a warrior and each new entrant
a David come to battle. And when it is over and you
are calling a hansom, what will the newsboy slip from

under his arm — a green *Westminster* or a pink *Globe* ? And at what time will the curtain rise on Lehar at Daly's ?

The nostalgia for cricket seems a kind of madness to those who have it not. They come late in life or from foreign parts willing to be instructed in the mysteries and, being instructed, are still inexpressibly bored ; they cannot understand what we see in the game. The answer is that it is not the game only that we see, but childhood and youth, and peace of mind in the recollection of enduring things :

> For the field is full of shades as I near the shadowy coast,
> And a ghostly batsman plays to the bowling of a ghost,
> And I look through my tears on a soundless-clapping host
> As the run-stealers flicker to and fro,
> > To and fro :—
> O my Hornby and my Barlow long ago !

A day at Lord's, with past welling up into the present, puts a bracket round controversy and gives imagination release. There are two minds — the mind that keeps its eye on the ball, and the mind that ranges. " So then the princess threw the ball at one of her company ; she missed the girl, and cast the ball into the deep. . . ." Whereupon, it will be remembered, all of them, being women, raised a piercing cry, and the goodly Odysseus awoke and sat up, and observed that another wicket had fallen, Trumper was out, and the Eighth Army had advanced on Carthage.

If not to St. John's Wood one might, of course, go to the National Gallery, though Trafalgar Square is too near the pelicans to be greatly sought for on a day off, and it is not every morning that, going up the steps in expectation of " The Entombment " or " The Haywain ", you find Renoir's lady in a brilliant necklace looking down at you from her stage-box. Or you may go to

Kew Gardens and stroll on the lawns there, or to Battersea
Park and rediscover the river and the line of Chelsea
without the Old Church, and that leads back to Sir
Thomas More and his Utopia, and may, if you are off
your guard, lead on to lesser men and theirs. Better that
Sir Thomas More should lead to Cicely Heron and she
to Holbein, and Holbein, when you are home again, to
taking down the long-neglected book that contains the
drawings of Ingres, for they are flawless, and that is
something in a wildly approximating world. They are,
if you will, " faultily faultless " like Andrea del Sarto's
painting. No doubt they miss something — and yet
Andrea was not for little men to sneer at, he who might
" bring the sweat " to Rafael's brow and correct his
drawing :

> To Rafael's ! — And indeed the arm is wrong.
> I hardly dare . . . yet, only you to see,
> Give the chalk here — quick, thus the line should go.

Ingres was of such a kind. And is there a fault, even of
perfection, in his drawing of Liszt ? Is there a miracle
of line to equal Paganini's fiddle ? What seems to matter
now, as much almost as the divine chances of genius,
is this unarguing devotion, this " useless " perfection, the
sense, communicated by Ingres, that to draw badly is
to sin and that to draw perfectly is to live well. While
that is believed, even of a pencil line, the world is not
sick unto death.

So the afternoon ends and, when tea has been taken
away, of all that day only the evening remains. Books,
idleness, the river, pictures, the Odyssey — have the hours
been wasted ? It must be confessed that the crime of
nostalgia has been flagrantly committed — or has even
this come to be considered, in recent months, less of a crime
than it was once supposed to be ? Civilization, as Whistler
might have said, is creeping up. The Middle West has

discovered Matthew Arnold, and a few of our most advanced blue-printers are hot upon the track of " Unto This Last ". Lord Keynes and Mr. Morgenthau are nearly level with Sir Thomas More on the subject of gold. And indeed history is not a means of excommunicating the past and sanctifying the future ; nor is nostalgia a vice unless it is a hankering for past things because they are past and not because they were good. It is a form of selectiveness in which emotion, which is sometimes poetry, fortifies the intellect's discernment, and, setting no locked dams across the tributaries of mankind, gives flow and unity to the epic. There is a nostalgia of the future as of the past, and a reconciliation between them, a fusing of them if only we can attain to it, seems to be what little wisdom we may have between hope and sadness.

The day is short ; the night comes ; and still, see how the artists love one another !

> But do not let us quarrel any more,
> No, my Lucrezia ; bear with me for once. . . .
> Eh ? the whole seems to fall into a shape
> As if I saw alike my work and self
> And all that I was born to be and do,
> A twilight-piece. . . .
> So free we seem, so fettered fast we are !

For many who were just old enough to fight in 1914 and are now again diverted from their proper life into some alien track, the twenty years' armistice was never more than an interval — to be valued the more because they knew how it would end. They counted the stars and said : "A June night, and no war !" In effect, they have been at war with Germany for twenty-eight years — and for how much longer if their minds were awake at Agadir ! It gives to past, present and future a powerful overlay. Childhood, boyhood, youth, maturity

— all, except childhood, look through one another, and childhood, like an imagined future, looks through them all.

> You smile ? Why, there's my picture ready made,
> There's what we painters call our harmony !

A day of leisure is not wasted that rediscovers the picture's proportion and what painters call its values. Not many may seem now to care greatly for a faultless line, but the past is an assurance that they will. Not many had a notion what one was talking about when ten, fifteen, twenty years ago one said : " A June night, and no war ! " But they understand now, as they stare at the balloons and the pelicans.

Is there not a sense in which it is true to say, not merely that the present must be interpreted by history but that neither present nor future can be imagined except through an imagining of the past ? Without this one is in peril of falling into a blind search for scapegoats. Either : " It is the fault of the rich " or " it is the apathy of the bourgeoisie " or " it is the naughtiness of socialism " — or, yet more sweepingly, " it is the folly of politicians ". Though a few selected heads might profitably fall, the search for group-scapegoats is always useless ; popular passion cannot analyse events or the causes of events with enough accuracy or justice. Fate is too large for our prejudices. It is as if a pack of landsmen in a cutter were to blame each other for rocking the boat when it is the sea that rocks them all. To understand that it is the sea that rocks us is the meaning of acceptance — which is so far from resignation or despair that it is the basis of good seamanship. Andrea del Sarto, not without bitterness, could cling to his dreaming integrity through all the rocking of the boat.

> While hand and eye and something of a heart
> Are left me, work's my ware, and what's it worth ?

I'll pay my fancy.   Only let me sit
The grey remainder of the evening out,
Idle, you call it, and muse perfectly
How I could paint, were I but back in France. . . .

Then, at the end of the day :

> I am grown peaceful as old age to-night.
> I regret little, I would change still less.
> Since there my past life lies, why alter it ?

And, finally, the great leap of the imagination :

> . . . What would one have ?
> In heaven, perhaps, new chances, one more chance —
> Four great walls in the New Jerusalem,
> Meted on each side by the angel's reed,
> For Leonard, Rafael, Angelo and me. . . .

Which means only that next morning on his way from
Fiesole to the Horse Guards, Andrea del Sarto thought
it still worth while to be an artist in this world and the
next. No one took much notice when he died and the
Servites buried him obscurely.

The Mighty
Strong Beast

THE name of Socrates is not one that would ordinarily be evoked by a defender of artists, for, if Plato is to be believed, he held a low opinion of them ; but he was at any rate gloriously intolerant of confused thinking, a hater of men who used popular catchwords without considering their meaning, and if he had listened to the long controversy about opening theatres on Sundays he might well have taken one of the controversialists by the lapel of his coat and said : " Tell me. What do you mean when you say that an actor is ' a servant of the public ' ? " The comfortable phrase is one in which the Sophists would have rejoiced, and Mr. Pecksniff after them ; that it should be used with so little pause for analysis on both sides of the actors' dispute is sadder and more important than the dispute itself, for the use of it implies a willingness among artists to accept a rule inapplicable to artists.

I might compare them [said Plato in a different context but in reference to the same principle] to a man who should study the tempers and tastes of a mighty strong beast who is fed by him. . . . Good he pronounces to be that in which the beast delights and evil to be that which he dislikes. . . . For when a man consorts with the many, and exhibits to them his poem or other work of art or the service which he has done to the State, making them his judges when he is not obliged, the so-called necessity of Diomede will oblige him to produce whatever they praise.

Like a philosopher, an artist must be continuously on his guard against the pretensions of the mighty strong beast to interfere with him, for nowadays the arts tempt the vulgar (it is Jowett's word) as strongly as philosophy tempted them when Plato wrote. In the following passage from " Republic VI ", Plato is speaking of philosophy, but what he says is, from our point of view, applicable to art :

Many are thus attracted by her whose natures are imperfect and whose souls are maimed and disfigured by their meannesses, as their bodies are by their trades and crafts. Is not this unavoidable ?

Yes.

Are they not exactly like a bald little tinker who has just got out of durance and come into a fortune ; he takes a bath and puts on a new coat, and is decked out as a bridegroom going to marry his master's daughter. . . . What will be the issue of such marriages ? Will they not be vile and bastard ?

There can be no question of it.

In brief, a philosopher or, in our world, an artist must not accept standards which are not his, or make the multitude his judges when he is not obliged, or subscribe to the saying that he is " a servant of the public " without examining it.

An artist, like other men, is a member of the community. Unless he is willing and able to dissociate himself from it — that is, to outlaw himself — he is bound by its laws ; for he exists, like other men, in more aspects than one ; he is not an artist only, but a father who desires protection for his children, or a traveller who benefits by the safety of the roads, or an islander who depends upon a system of sea-transport which the community provides, and he must pay to the community what it justly requires of him. But this is not to say that he must produce whatever the multitude desire or that he is their servant. A man who contributes to a common labour does not become the servant of the majority of his fellow-labourers.

The question becomes, then : what may the community justly require of a man in return for the services he accepts from it ? The answer depends, first, upon the view we take of the community. If it is, as our enemies teach, a mystical unit, if men are to be thought of as existing only as part of it and not in themselves or in an individual relationship to God, it follows logically that there are no limits to the community's demand, for it possesses all of each man ; he is not even so separate as to be its slave or servant, he is *of* it and is completed in it ; but if once this total view be repudiated, it becomes clear that some of the community's demands are to be considered as just but others as unjust, and an attempt to distinguish between them must be made.

It might be supposed that no demand more excessive or unjust could be made upon a man than that he should take his own life as penalty for having committed an offence which he himself considered an exercise of virtue ; but Socrates, of whom this demand was made, accepted it and refused to make his escape when he might have done so. Though the sentence of death was, in his view, wrong, he believed, for the reasons given in the " Phaedo ", that he would be wrong not to consent to it. Much earlier, though he was no lover of war and had better things to do with his life than march in armies, he fought as Tolstoy did. The familiar passage of the " Symposium " which describes his winter campaigning when he and Alcibiades were fellow-soldiers before Potidaea comes back to mind upon thought of the Russian winter, for Alcibiades tells how

whilst the frost was intolerably severe, and no one went out of their tents, or if they went out, wrapped themselves up carefully and put fleeces upon their feet, and bound their legs with hairy skins, Socrates went out only with the same cloak on that he usually wore, and walked barefoot upon the ice—

an extremely irritating habit, like so many others of that great man, but evidence at any rate that he did not shirk the common hardship. He would fight, he would obey the laws, he would die in submission to the State's decree ; if ever there was a man to whom that begging and benighted word " anti-social " did not apply he was Socrates ; and yet there was a point at which he stuck, repudiating in advance the authority of the " mighty strong beast ". It is worth while to observe where, in him, obedience ended and absolute resistance began.

" But I do know that injustice and disobedience to a better, whether God or man, is evil and dishonourable," he said to his judges, and yet, he added, there was one command he would not accept from them. If they were to say to him that they would let him go, but on condition that he was " not to inquire and speculate in this way any more ", then he would reply : " Men of Athens, I honour and love you ; but I shall obey God rather than you, and while I have life and strength I shall never cease. . . . Either acquit me or not ; but whichever you do, understand that I shall never alter my ways, not even if I have to die many times." Church's translation adds emphasis to Jowett's : " Be sure that I shall not alter my way of life ; no, not if I have to die for it many times ".

This is the answer that all artists have to make in private and in public continually. As men and women, they are loyal citizens ; as artists, they are the servants neither of the public nor of their own comfort and safety. If a conflict arises between the two loyalties, the man must be prepared to suffer, as Socrates did, that the philosopher, the artist, the truth-bearer in him may not be perjured. It is one of the tests of good government and of a true sense of values in a community that such conflicts shall seldom arise and, if they arise, shall not be forced to bitter conclusions ; for a wise community recognizes that different men contribute to the general good in different ways, some directly by supplying urgent wants of which all are conscious, and some indirectly by being, in their lives and work, witnesses to beauty and truth.

It is among the proofs of civilization in a modern community that the majority in it should be capable of making this distinction and of maintaining it even in times of stress and passion. In England we have struggled. for this and have gone some way towards attaining it. Although there are many thousands, perhaps millions, who personally attach no importance to the work of priests, no one suggests that they should be conscribed. Although almost the whole population feels that men who are physically capable of it should fight, the validity of genuinely conscientious refusal to fight is recognized by law and tolerated by opinion. The argument is roughly this : " I disagree with the man. I think he ought to fight. But I recognize that by fighting he would, in his own view, be disobeying an authority higher than that of the Athenians ; therefore I cannot reasonably persecute him." This is not the language of the " mighty strong beast " requiring that its every pleasure be satisfied.

The English are often blind, often insensitive, lazy or stubborn as the strong beast is, but they are very little persecutors ; and they have another quality which distinguishes them from him — a respect for law and an absolute acceptance, contrary even to their own prejudices, of the judges' interpretation of it. So far is this carried that whenever the executive, which after all holds its place by will of the majority, is overridden by the bench, ordinary Englishmen, instead of complaining, often rejoice exceedingly. Why? Is not the Government of their own choosing ? Why do they enjoy seeing it checked by the Courts ? The answer seems to be that they regard the judges as protectors of individual liberties. Parliament and the executive may represent the popular mood at the last election, but the Law is felt to be a distillation of the people's mature will. It is, so to speak, a safeguard against the tyrannies that a rash majority may sometimes commit ; it puts the mighty strong beast on a chain.

One does not need to be a waver of flags or to blind oneself to the popular faults of the English in order to believe that among all the fallible multitudes which are, or have been, upon earth, they have as good a claim as any to the virtue of compassionate justice. This virtue depends upon a power or at any rate a wish to see into men's hearts when judging their acts, and to value them for what they are in themselves and not only for their apparent usefulness to the multitude. So the soldier does not hastily condemn the non-resister or the agnostic despise the priest. This is our distinguishing tolerance, a noble and difficult one, which our people have inherited from the past. Yet, in one respect, we are strangely wanting. To other minorities we give, or try to give, the benefit of their own point of view, but seldom to artists. We do not persecute them as men ; we measure out to them the same justice that we offer to barmen or railway porters, and in this seeming justice our injustice lies ; for whereas we admit a special category of priests, another of non-resisters and another of doctors, allowing to each its own privilege, we admit no special category of artists. We applaud them when they do what we want ; sometimes we idolize them as they neither desire nor deserve ; then suddenly, when a dispute touches their life as artists, we stifle reason with some such blanketing catchword as that they are " servants of the public ". Two deeply relevant questions go unasked : what is an artist? and what *therefore* is his place in the community ?

They are always left unasked when dispute arises

about the opening of theatres on Sundays. Stage-hands, chorus-girls and actors of the first rank are bracketed together in the public mind and argued about in the public print as if they were all indistinguishable members of an industry which had no other responsibility than to serve the mighty strong beast. No one seriously inquires how the proposed change may affect the theatre as an art. Perhaps it may not affect it at all, perhaps benefit it, perhaps cause it to deteriorate — which? The question is highly technical, and my purpose here is not to answer but to demonstrate the need to ask it, for, if it is not asked in this theatrical context, how shall it be asked in any other? If we are prepared to conclude that because waitresses, bus-conductors and journalists work on Sundays actors should be compelled to do likewise, we accept as a premise that actors are in the same category with waitresses, bus-conductors and journalists. The theatre then becomes an equivalent of the transport and catering industries, painters on canvas become the same, from the civic point of view, as house-painters, and literature is to be thought of only as a supplier of public demand. The point is not a trivial one. An actor is an artist as well as an employee in a trade. If we fail to distinguish the artistic quality in him or to recognize that this quality implies a distinct way of life carrying with it distinct responsibilities and privileges, we become guilty of the same failure in our estimate of all artists. When art is considered as a branch of the catering industry, then indeed the mighty strong beast is let loose.

Or perhaps that is how art ought to be considered? Perhaps the notion that artists, like priests or doctors, are entitled to the community's special consideration is anti-social? If they claim, as Socrates did, the privilege of self-determination, of non-obedience to the majority within their own way of life, certainly they must show that, in return for that privilege, they accept a rare responsibility and perform a special duty. They must show also that their discharge of this duty in their own way has its place not only among the values of the past but among those of the present, for one of the voices of the Beast may roar that individualistic art has had its day. Every approach to this subject leads back to the same question : what, by reason of his art, is an artist's place in the community ?

There are many ways in which it may be answered — by showing, for example, why it is true to say that an artist is a link, a means of communication, between the universal and the particular and so a power to give unity to the human personality, but to emphasize this aspect of his service would be to set foot in metaphysical territory which cannot now be explored. The simpler answer is that an artist is, in his nature, the antithesis of the mighty strong beast — a corrective of the evils to which a democratic society is exposed. The peril of all democracies, which increases as they come nearer and nearer to being purely numerical democracies with no brake upon the impulse of a majority, is that among them absolute values may gradually be made to look ridiculous. Everything, men begin to say, " is relative " — a vague, tolerant-sounding phrase which often means no more than : " there is no point at which I will stand, there is no concession I will not make to popular opinion, there is nothing for which now and always I am willing to fight and die ".

To an artist such a phrase is completely unacceptable. As a man, he will like other men make concessions and, outside his art, will do what the community requires of him, but, within the area of his art, he, like a priest, acknowledges allegiance to no man and no State. He will sweep a crossing or fight a war, but he will not, as an actor, give a bad performance or, as a painter, paint a bad picture. Nor — and here is the heart of controversy — will he do those things which may lead to the deterioration of his art. What are these things? To suspend the practice of his art while he makes a journey or fights a war is not one of them, for this is only to lessen his production, not to corrupt it; but to change his way of life in submission to a set of values not primarily aesthetic is in him the equivalent of a soldier's accepting a bribe from the enemy or of a priest's betraying the confessional. Against this he must stand firm or perish. To dishonour him and his saving absolutism is to put all values in jeopardy, for, like Socrates, he compels the mighty strong beast to pause, to ask itself questions, and so imposes those limits upon its power which distinguish a democracy from a mob.

Tolstoy :
" War and Peace "

WHAT is " War and Peace " ? * It is not a novel, even less is it a poem, and still less a historical chronicle. . . . The words have scarcely been read when a thousand readers leap up to protest against the inclusion of three such heresies in a sentence. How pernickety and perverse has criticism become which can say in this context : it is not a novel ! Have not a score of pundits agreed to call it the greatest novel ever written ? And if it is not a novel or a poem or a chronicle, what is it ? This is the question that Tolstoy was asking ; he, if anyone, is perverse, heretical and pernickety ; for the dangerous sentence is his own — only the inverted commas were for a convenient moment omitted.

His comment was made and published in 1868, while the work itself was alive in him, for its last two volumes did not come from the press until the following year. Long afterwards, when his view of art had changed and he was bent upon making the whole world — even the world he had created — conform in his mind to the social morality of his later period, he believed himself to have thought differently. " In ' War and Peace '," he said, " I loved the people's emotions arising from the war of 1812. . . . I strove to write a history of the people." Compare this with the continuation of his early (1868) apologia. When the first part of his book appeared, some people had told him that the character of the period was " not sufficiently defined ". By this they seem to have meant what a modern critic would mean if he were

---

* " War and Peace ", by Leo Tolstoy. Translated by Louise and Aylmer Maude, with an Introduction by Aylmer Maude.

to say that Tolstoy's point of view was too aristocratic, that he laid too little emphasis on the tyranny of class. " I know," he writes, " what ' the characteristics of the period ' are that people do not find in my novel — the horrors of serfdom, the immuring of wives, the flogging of grown-up sons . . . and so on ", and, having defended himself against this charge by claiming that to emphasize these violences would have been to distort the truth, he adds quietly :

That period had its own characteristics (as every epoch has), which resulted from the predominant alienation of the upper class from other classes, from the religious philosophy of the time, from peculiarities of education, from the habit of using the French language, and so forth. That is the characteristic I tried to depict as well as I could.

This is very different from saying : " I strove to write a history of the people ", unless the word " people " be understood in its most inclusive sense.

" War and Peace ", then, is not a novel or a poem or a historical chronicle or a Marxian document. What is it ? There is a sense in which it is true to say that it is a gigantic improvisation upon a double theme, but, if we are to say that, we must be careful that the word " improvisation " is not misunderstood and that our submission in regard to the double theme is clearly defined. Tolstoy was not improvising in the sense of his being, as an artist, careless, or of his having arrogantly assumed that aesthetic form was unimportant. His improvisation consisted in his power to turn to his book's advantage the circumstance by which so many books, particularly long books, have been ruined — namely, that the man who began and the man who finished it were not the same man. The form he chose was so elastic or, strictly, so plastic, that it was not broken by but continually responded to the changes in the writer, so that he was never cabined by it, never tied down in what he was about to say by what he had already said, and, in his own words, left each day " a bit of my flesh in the ink-stand ". As for the double theme, it will be enough for the moment to say that what I have in mind is not the split between the personal story and the national saga that Percy Lubbock's brilliant analysis distinguished, but a theme that is double as a flawless marriage is double, and productive of unity, as such a marriage may be, in spite of great divergences of interest and subject. What has been called improvisation, and the unity arising from a dualism of theme, have, in fact, the same roots. Discussion of one and discussion of the other are the same discussion. It is one of the chief difficulties of seeing the book as a whole that they must be taken in order.

As one reads again this huge work, a feeling of Tolstoy's presence within it is continuous and urgent. Not only the scenes of love and the scenes of war, but even the historical disquisitions are hot with his personality. His historical method is as far as possible removed from the methods of Flaubert on the one hand and of Stendhal on the other ; it is neither objective nor ironic nor romantic, but a projection of himself into the historical material, an impregnation of it by himself, so that whether he is describing an Emperor or a battle, or is turning aside from story-telling to put the historians in their place, the glow of his persuasion, his eagerness — yes, if you like, his wrongheadedness — is always in the writing. There, in piles, were his documents, his notes, his plans. No doubt, when he went to bed each night, he knew, or thought he knew, what he would write next day. So, in a sense, he did. But in the night, waking and sleeping, his imagination had run on, his theory of pre-determination in history had thrown out a new branch, he himself had changed, and when he came again to his desk it was always that change which he impressed upon his work. Other writers' self-discipline often consists — and ought to consist — in keeping themselves within the original plan, the premeditated form, of their work ; this is not mere consistency, which is no great virtue, but is a means of intensification — a valuable means, as Shakespeare and Wordsworth knew when they chose to write sonnets because, in this formal confinement, they found a liberation of spirit. Tolstoy's self-discipline was different in kind, but was still self-discipline. He was no careless, sprawling profligate of his genius, writing on and on with eyeball rolling and in defiance of measure. His self-discipline — and it was the struggle of his personal life long after he had lost interest in it as an aesthetic struggle — was of the kind that looks for its reward, as Pierre looked for his, in the unselfconsciousness of being true to oneself. If Tolstoy had pruned away those historical disquisitions, if he had said : " these are tedious, these must go " or " I am telling a story and these have no part in it ", he would have ceased to be true to himself, for the subject of the historical disquisition *was* himself that morning. He was bound to improvise because it was through the complex network of his improvisation (as it was in Turgenev through the strict channel of premeditated form) that his vitality flowed. Tolstoy's divagations from his tale can be as infuriating as his later tracts — but infuriating they are, never flat, never toneless ; and how often, after a sentence or two, irritation passes, the deserted narrative is forgotten, the divagation establishes itself, the wisdom (or the perversity) of the improvisation carries the reader away ! Pierre, it will be remembered, had a habit, extremely Tolstoyan, of talking and thinking about one thing while Natásha was talking and thinking about another :

" Do you know what I am thinking about ? " she asked. " About Platón Karatáev. Would he have approved of you now, do you think ? "

Pierre was not at all surprised at this question. He understood his wife's line of thought.

" Platón Karatáev ? " he repeated, and pondered, evidently sincerely trying to imagine Karatáev's opinion on the subject. " He would not have understood. . . . yet perhaps he would."

" I love you awfully ! " Natásha suddenly said. " Awfully, awfully ! "

Now, how did Tolstoy know that she would suddenly say that ? The knowledge was part of the unselfconscious intuition which enabled him to risk, as no one else would have dared to risk, a sagging of his reader's interest. Like Pierre, he could risk anything as long as he was true to his own improvisations. They are not what the reader expects or desires, but they are, even in their faults, a passionate expression of Tolstoy himself. " I love you awfully ! " Natásha exclaims, and indeed there is nothing else to say.

The same gift of improvisation, the same power to evoke love by the exercise of that gift, is even more conspicuous in the personal, than in the philosophical, passages of this unique book. Criticism has never tired of remarking the masterly ease with which Tolstoy gives life to each scene, but has sometimes been content to ascribe to this quality, common to the epic and the domestic or romantic aspects of " War and Peace ", the sense of unity and rightness that is its effect. But we must go further than this. It is not enough to say that Tolstoy writes so well that he covers the joins or at any rate dazzles the reader to them. The point to make is that his glamour and his realism differed in kind, and not in degree only, from the glamour and realism of other masters. The early scene of the little girl, Natásha, in the conservatory with Boris, because it is as familiar as any, may serve as an example. If anything is certain among the admitted perils of criticism from internal evidence, it is that, in writing this scene, Tolstoy was, in his own special sense, improvising. An imaginative writer cannot be asked a more difficult question than : " Are your characters portraits ? Are they derived from particular persons ? " The answer is always " Yes ", and with equal truth, " I don't know ". This would have been Tolstoy's answer if the question had been put to him with regard to Natásha and his young sister-in-law, Tanya. Sometimes Natásha was Tanya in his mind, and, to the extent that she was Tanya, whatever man was at the moment in emotional relationship with Natásha became, as it were, impregnated by the personality of Tolstoy. No one would suggest that, in the book's ordinary course, Boris was an autobiographical character ; for the most part, Tolstoy's treatment of him is objective and detached ; so no doubt he intended it to be when he planned the fifth chapter of Book One ; but when suddenly the little girl jumped on to a tub "to be higher than he" and "embraced him so that both her slender bare arms clasped him above his neck, and tossing back her hair, kissed him full on the lips ", Tolstoy departed from his plan (Boris has been a little dull until this moment and will be dull again) and threw in one of his supreme improvisations, vitalizing Boris by the miraculous process of pouring himself into that hitherto dim young man.

" Natásha," he said, " you know that I love you, but . . ."
" You are in love with me ? " Natásha broke in.
" Yes, I am, but please don't let us do like that. . . . In another four years . . . then I will ask for your hand."
Natásha considered.
" Thirteen, fourteen, fifteen, sixteen," she counted on her slender little fingers. " All right ! Then it's settled ? "
A smile of joy and satisfaction lit up her eager face.
" Settled ! " replied Boris.
" For ever ? " said the little girl. " Till death itself ? "

It is not necessary to be aware of the subtle and tender relationship between Tolstoy and Tanya, whom he knew when she was of this age, to feel the personal entry of the writer into this scene, or to be sure that it was improvised, unselfconscious — so unselfconscious that, if Tolstoy had afterwards been asked whether the scene was partly autobiographical, he might have answered " Yes ", and with equal truth, " I don't know ". It is one of the scenes that are written " in the sleep of the artist ", though every word may be deliberately chosen and as deliberately revised. To write in this way was Tolstoy's loveliest gift. He could apply it, as no one else has ever done, to everything — to an historical disquisition so that its substantial " dullness " was made to glow by the heat of himself in it, to a drawing-room, a race-meeting, a drunken party, to endowing Anna Karénina with a femininity that outshines any in literature, to giving to Natásha's kiss a lightness, a passion, an actuality that stop the heart.

To what, in this book, was he applying this great and unifying power ? It is the old question : what is " War and Peace " ? After he has told us that it is not a novel or a poem or a chronicle, Tolstoy tries to tell us what it is : " ' War and Peace ' is what the author wished and was able to express in the form in which it is expressed. Such an announcement of disregard of conventional form in an artistic production might seem presumptuous were it premeditated. . . ." This is all we are told. The passage is at first obscure, but if it is considered in the light of what has already been said of " unselfconscious improvisation ", is it not suddenly full of meaning ? There were two things that " the author wished and was able to express " : himself in his relation to individual men and women, and his sense of values in society considered historically. These are the two themes, and they are one theme. Because they are two, and are to be treated on a gigantic scale, there is a seeming split in the book. And yet they are one because a man's sense of values is himself and changes with him. It is the product of his experience and his opinions, and it was this *product* that " the author wished to express " and " was able to express " not in the conventional form of the novel but only in an " unpremeditated " social and historical improvisation.

Here, then, is the split which readers have perceived, and here the essential unity which they have felt. This dualism has always made hard the analytical as well as the impressionistic criticism of " War and Peace " and perhaps lies at the root of the difficulty of some readers who find in it a certain forbidding confusion. The confusion exists, but it is resolved for a reader who discovers that what he is asked to do is not to receive a single impression of Tolstoy's genius at a given time but to grow with him, to yield to change as he yields to it, to respond to his improvisations. As he wrote, he was moving towards the crisis in his life which is called his conversion. We are confronted with the paradox that, while he was writing a masterpiece, his mind was preparing a revolution of his aesthetic and moral values. Soon the two aspects of himself, the artist and the teacher, were to separate ; the seeds of division are in " War and Peace ", but as yet the division has not come ; the marriage — if one may so speak of the alliance between the two impulses of Tolstoy's genius — survives, but it is, like the marriage of Natásha and Pierre, a union of two very different beings, and there is tension in it. When Natásha and Pierre were alone together, they " began to talk as only a husband and wife can talk . . . different subjects were talked about at one and the same time ". Nevertheless, " this simultaneous discussion of many topics did not prevent a clear understanding, but on the contrary was the surest sign that they fully understood one another ". What was dangerous to them, as it was to Tolstoy, was an excess of logic. They were safest, as he was, when they improvised without self-consciousness. " When he began proving anything or talking argumentatively and calmly, and she, led on by his example, began to do the same, she knew that they were on the verge of a quarrel." The prophetic analogy with Tolstoy's own life is almost intolerably close. Soon by talking argumentatively and seeking always to prove something, he was to destroy the marriage of his wisdom with his art. He was to ask " What is Art ? " and return a moralist's answer ; and never again was Natásha, upon an impulse, to cry out " I love you awfully ! " or to kiss him full on the lips.

Tolstoy :
The Second Epilogue

I

THE Second Epilogue to " War and Peace " bears closely upon the problems of the twentieth century, for its subject is the forces that move nations and the relationship between free will and necessity in the history of mankind. Many have probably been withheld from reading it, or at any rate from reading it to the end, by the tiresomeness of Tolstoy's approach to the heart of his subject — a tiresomeness frequent in him when he turned from narrative towards the pulpit. Once fairly in the pulpit, he was never dull, but he had a habit, while on his way there, of quibbling with his opponents — in this case, historians whose interpretation of history differed from his own — in a way that is exasperating to those who love his genius and hate to see it spent in the verbal twisting of other men's tails. But with Tolstoy one must always continue. As if a lion should pride himself on his skill in catching mice — an accomplishment in which every tabby is his superior — Tolstoy delighted to believe that he was a strict logician, and there are many passages in his works devoted to dialectical mouse-catching. Even when the mouse has made its escape down the wide hole of a fallacy he still thinks that he has it under his paw, and, in that belief, goes through the motions of triumphantly worrying and playing with it. Nevertheless one must stay with Tolstoy. Always, after a little while, he forgets the mouse, and is up and away through the great forest of his imagination after larger game.

There is a double interest in following him. First, there is a biographical interest, for here is the germ of

Tolstoy's ultimate philosophy, of that unique mingling of non-resistance with anarchism which, being pressed to a logical extreme, led the old lion into a trap ; and here, secondly, is an indication that the trap consisted in his failure to distinguish clearly between groups that are evil and groups that are good. And this is a subject that desperately concerns us to-day, whether we are, in the non-party sense, communistic by temperament, seeking good through leagues, associations and groups, or whether we are by nature individualistic and have to check in ourselves an irrational tendency to tar all groups with the same brush. To both kinds of man, the Second Epilogue is exceedingly instructive. Not so much in itself as in its implications, it leads to a remarkable impasse — the very impasse by which both individualistic thinkers and communistic thinkers are threatened if they press their theory to an extreme. The purpose of the first part of this essay is to examine the Second Epilogue from an individualistic point of view ; to show how its argument may lead to a belief that the formation of groups is a prime cause of war ; and then to say : " But this is the logic that was to bring the old lion into a trap ! Beware of it. Match it with experience. Have not you fallen, and did not Tolstoy fall, into the error of confusing groups that are evil with groups that are good ? " And the purpose of the essay's second part will be to seek this necessary distinction between two things which are nowadays wrongly, and often bitterly, confused.

Tolstoy's theory of history was even more unorthodox than the philosophical conclusions which sprang from it. He did not believe that the will of either Napoleon or Alexander was the cause of the events of their day ; and he felt that not only the biographical historians, who said that this was so, but the universal historians and the cultural historians as well were fundamentally wrong.

It was, for him, false to say that troops had crossed the
Niemen because Napoleon had ordered them to cross it,
and equally false to suggest that Frenchmen had drowned
and killed one another because certain books had been
written or certain ideas been put into limited circulation
by Rousseau or Chateaubriand or Madame de Staël.
An economic interpretation of history would have satisfied him as little. His own view he summarized thus :

The movement of nations is caused not by power, nor by
intellectual activity, nor even by a combination of the two
as historians have supposed, but by the activity of *all* the
people who participate in the events, and who always combine in such a way that those taking the largest direct share
in the event take on themselves the least responsibility and
vice versa.

Then, comparing men in their multiplicity to particles of
matter which are subject to natural laws, he approached
the question of the existence or non-existence of historical
laws. Just as we cannot say why the interaction of heat
and electricity occurs, but know that it does occur " and
that it is a law ", so we do not know why war and
revolution occur, but " only know that to produce the one
or the other action people combine in a certain formation
in which they all take part ", and we say " that it is a
law ". If history dealt with external phenomena, this
simple and obvious law would suffice and the argument
would be over. But the law of history relates to man.

A particle of matter cannot tell us that it does not feel
the law of attraction or repulsion and that that law is untrue,
but man, who is the subject of history, says plainly : " I am
free, and am therefore not subject to the law ". The presence
of the problem of man's free will, though unexpressed, is felt
at every step of history.

When Tolstoy reached this point, two-thirds of the
Epilogue were written. The mice were forgotten. The

lion was at full-stretch, magnificently hunting the problem of the exercise of free will within the conditions of historical necessity.

Tolstoy's thought, in this matter, had its centre in the French Revolution and the Napoleonic wars. How had the nations been moved to so much waste and such wild contradictions ? His argument strikes deep. Considered as a contribution to the theory of history (which is what it set out to be), it is definite and constructive ; but considered as a criticism of life, it leads to a gigantic question mark.

He asks whether the life of humanity should properly be regarded as the result of the free, or as the result of the constrained, activity of man. From the point of view of reasoned observation " man is subject to the law of necessity ", but those who argue from this that the soul and freedom do not exist — or, as our modern jargon goes, that man is an " economic animal " — are as stupid as those who, in Tolstoy's own day, were saying that the soul and free will could not exist " because at an unknown period of time we sprang from apes ". It is pleasant to see how hot Tolstoy could be against the " advanced " — that is to say, the pseudo-scientific thinkers of his time :

Only in our self-confident day of the popularization of knowledge — thanks to that most powerful engine of ignorance, the diffusion of printed matter — has the question of the freedom of will been put on a level on which the question itself cannot exist. In our time the majority of so-called advanced people — that is, the crowd of ignoramuses — have taken the work of the naturalists who deal with one side of the question for a solution of the whole problem.

So have the " so-called advanced people " of our day taken the work of the economists, who deal with one side of the question, for a solution of the whole problem. Tolstoy would have none of this partiality of judgment.

Free will and inevitability were for him no more mutually exclusive than religion and scientific observation. He showed, first, that neither complete freedom nor complete necessity was conceivable. "Only by uniting them do we get a clear conception of man's life." And so he proceeded to his conclusion that—

If history has for its object the study of the movement of the nations and of humanity, and not the narration of episodes in the lives of individuals, it, too [like the natural sciences], setting aside the conception of cause, should seek the laws common to all the inseparably interconnected infinitesimal elements of free will.

He made no attempt to give general statement to these laws, but this much is clear : for him, the force that moves nations — that is, the determining historical force — is the resultant of two other forces : that of free will and that of necessity. The force of necessity, compelling man to drown and kill, springs not from the will of Dynasts and Leaders but from a fateful quality inherent in the nature of man himself — a quality " common to all the infinitesimal elements of free will ". Our exercise of free will is not cancelled, but is conditioned and enveloped, by this necessity. Our freedom is, as it were, the freedom of a mariner to use sail or helm while voyaging upon the stream of necessity. This figure is consistent with Tolstoy's view of the Dynasts and the Führers. They are in the same boat with us ; no will of theirs or ours can lift it out of the stream. The mystery is that the stream has its origin, direction and strength in our own nature. There are, Tolstoy contends, laws, which history must seek, governing the relationship between man's necessity and his free will. Men are compelled by something in ourselves. Not by Napoleon, not by Hitler. Not by the men of ideas — Rousseau or Karl Marx or Tolstoy himself. Men are compelled, or made subject to compulsion, by what? By their fateful habit of ceasing to act as responsible individuals and of organizing themselves in groups. Reconsider Tolstoy's own words, already quoted : " The movement of nations ", he says, " is caused . . . by the activity of *all* the people . . . who always combine in such a way that those taking the largest direct share in the event take on themselves the least responsibility." We know to what this doctrine led Tolstoy, how it affected his whole theory of government, and induced in him a death-struggle between his logical and his intuitive consciences. He was doubly divided. As an aristocrat and an artist, he was intensely individualistic ; as a philanthropist, he was communally minded as few have ever been ; and yet, as a philosophical historian, an analyst of masses, he perceived that " the more our activity is connected with other people the less free it is." Drawn towards groups by his philanthropy, he was repelled from them by his knowledge that they were the instrument of man's self-subjugation. They were, so to speak, the wire through which the current of power ran between the enslaved masses and the equally enslaved Leaders — equally enslaved because, as he said, he was " unable to attribute importance to the actions of those who thought they controlled events ". A consciousness of free will, Tolstoy repeated again and again with troubled emphasis, is inherent in us, and yet " taking a wide view of history we are indubitably convinced of a sempiternal law by which events occur ". And the implication of all his writing on the subject is that this law which caused millions of people to kill one another when it was " clear to each of them that this could not benefit any of them " operated in Napoleon's day and will always operate through men's fateful tendency to combine. " Why war and revolution occur," says Tolstoy, " we do not know. We only know that to produce the one or the other action people combine in a certain formation." And again : " How is it that millions of men commit collective crimes ? . . . Is there any collective action which cannot find its justification in political unity, in patriotism, in the balance of power, or in civilization ? "

To review this argument to-day is to find much confirmation of it in the history of the world since Tolstoy's death. Man's tendency to combine, whether in racial groups or in totalitarian parties, has never been responsible for so much cruelty and waste. The temptation to press the argument to a logical extreme is very strong. For a moment let us yield to the temptation and see to what it leads.

If there is a necessity, a predetermination, producing this disastrous effect upon mankind, and if there is a law in this matter comparable with the natural laws, we are compelled to ask whether there are, in human nature, any constant and universal elements upon which such a law might rest. What is there in man that is certain, fixed, necessitous, independent of his free will ? Even his need to satisfy appetites is in such a degree governable as to be an unsure foundation of law. Certainly he is born, certainly he dies — is anything else certain ? or may we deduce from these certainties any conclusions which, though not absolute, are so nearly absolute that they may be regarded as stepping-stones towards a law ? The key to the problem seems to be in men's certainty that they must die, which produces in them a desire to transcend death, manifested in the religious and in the reproductive instincts. These are near-absolutes. It produces also — and here we are approaching an explanation of why men " drown and kill " one another and subject themselves to Dynasts — a desire to intensify life itself. Why should a desire to intensify life lead to " drowning and killing " ? Because it leads men, according to their temperaments, to do one of two things :

either, if they fear solitude, to organize themselves in groups and masses and find refuge from solitude in submission to leadership; or, if they are by temperament individualistic, to be hedged into external submission by their passionate longing for inward peace. "Yes, yes," they say, " I will do what you want, I will cross the Niemen or accept Louis XVIII, or follow Bonaparte when he returns from Elba — I will do any of these things because to do them is a less interference with my personal life than actively to refuse to do them."

Thus groups or regiments or armies or parties are continually formed and reformed about those few exceptional and troublesome human beings, called Dynasts or Leaders, whose desire to intensify their own lives or to transcend death takes the form of organizing group-exploits, the purpose of which is sometimes called " emancipation ", sometimes " glory ", sometimes " fraternity " and sometimes " revenge ", but which have all the same characteristic : that they extend the area of necessity in human life by diminishing the area of free will. It seems then that an element common to all men has emerged — their tendency, in the knowledge of death, to form or to accept the formation of groups, and that this tendency, however noble or self-sacrificial its motive may appear to be, is fatal because it gives to Dynasts their material, gives it to one Leader after another, to one revolutionary after another, and, Tolstoy would have added, to one government after another, and is responsible for what he pointed out as the illogical and contradictory violences of history.

Granted Tolstoy's premises, this is the logical conclusion of his argument. The more men become " group-conscious " instead of, in the original sense, self-conscious, the greater is their surrender of free will, the less influence do they exert upon the course of history, the more are they dominated by a necessity or fate external to themselves. Organization in any form must appear, if regarded in this Tolstoyan light, as a repudiation of the individual's moral responsibility, and, therefore, as evil. In this gigantic paradox, there is profound truth to which the contemporary world has been increasingly blind, but it is a truth which leads to frustration and despair unless it be qualified by an attempt to distinguish between groups that are evil and groups that are good.

II

Faced by a knowledge of physical death, men have two tendencies seemingly opposed : the individualistic and the social. Both are subject to perversion and abuse. The individualistic way of life, which may degenerate into selfishness, is at its highest an attempt, amid the confusion and distraction of crowded mortality, to intensify and purify spiritual life while still in the body. The social tendency is distinct from this, though not in truth opposed to it, and is expressed in the organization of groups. These groups have many forms — the tribe, the family, the village community, the religious congregation — but all have, in the knowledge of death, a common origin. Some groups have their proximate cause in the instinct of self-preservation ; thus men band themselves together in arms or in agricultural communities. Families spring from the reproductive instinct ; religious communities from a desire to have assurance of life beyond the body. The division of motive is not rigid. As society has become more complex, group has intermingled with group and motive with motive in such a way as to make distinction hard. It may, therefore, be of the more value, in an attempt to discover what groups are good and what perverse, to keep two things in mind : first, to how great an extent the natural association of men in groups was, in one form or another, their attempted answer to physical death ; and, secondly, that herein is the unbreakable link between the social and the individualistic ways of life. Both are rooted in the religious instinct ; both are rooted in the instinct of self-preservation, the individualist happening to prefer the protective method of the snail to that of the ant. A group altogether divorced from these origins may be expected to become perverse and, in its development, corrupt and dangerous ; to become what Tolstoy conceived of groups as being — an instrument of destructive fate, causing men to " drown and kill " one another contrary to their interest and free will.

" Her conclusion was ", says E. M. Forster of one of his characters in " Howards End ", " that any human being lies nearer to the unseen than any organization, and from this she never varied." This was Tolstoy's conclusion also, and is scarcely to be gainsaid except by those who deny either the existence of the unseen or its importance. Nevertheless it remains true that there are many — indeed, a great majority of mankind — who find, as a fact of experience, that they are helped in their approach to the unseen by making it in company. An organization is necessary to the exercise of their religious instinct, and it is impossible to consider unnatural or perverse a community which satisfies this need in themselves. Whether we agree or disagree with the doctrine of the community they choose — that is to say, whether its way of approach to the unseen happens to be our own — is completely irrelevant. An association of men which exists to enable the religious instinct of its members may fall into what we consider error and commit what we consider crimes, but it is not, as a group and in its nature, perverse. But it may change its nature while preserving its form. Tolstoy did not cease to point out that groups are the instruments of power. Even the most innocent religious community may become such an instrument, and, in proportion as it does so, cease to be an enablement of man's religious instinct and become a limitation upon it. From the internal tension thus created arise religious cleavage and religious war. The group becomes coercive and proselytizing, and so dangerous.

Nevertheless we know and, unless we are fanatical individualists, must recognize that men who are " helped in their approach to the unseen by making it in company " require, as a condition of that help, a certain order or discipline. A group is not to be condemned because it provides this discipline, either directly or by an accumulation of custom from which order arises naturally. Who does not feel, as he reads Pater's account of the private Ambarvalia and of Marius's part in the ceremonies of that day, that something has been lost to life since then ? We have laid aside too much of the pleasant ritualistic divisions of life, which arise from the interplay of common existence and common faith — festivals that renew the heart, the celebration of days and seasons, the changes of dress and song and mood which, from time to time throughout the year, our forefathers made in company, until men arose to teach them that their various wisdom was irrational. Marius also knew that a part of what he did was irrational. He was disgusted by " the central act of the sacrifice itself, a piece of everyday butcher's work, such as we decorously hide out of sight ", but the country ceremony, in which all the little community and even the dead had a share, refreshed him, and simple things — bread, oil, wine, milk —

regained for him, by their use in such religious service, that poetic and as it were moral significance, which surely belongs to all the means of daily life, could we but break through the veil of our familiarity with things by no means vulgar in themselves.

Only the gentle discipline of communal custom can enable that " veil of our familiarity " to be broken through, and the process, which some would call super-stitious and others trivial, is neither of these, but genuinely religious, and a justification of the group that enables it. Again and again the same words — " enable ", " enablement ", " permissiveness " — return as marks of virtue in a group. Are we to conclude that as soon as a group ceases to enable individual freedom, to extend spiritual perception, to cultivate and protect the exercise of free will, it is in danger of being corrupted ?

Before resting upon such a conclusion it is necessary to approach the problem from a different angle — to see it from the point of view of those who sincerely believe in the efficacy of collective action to set right the wrongs of the world. Some of these, however sincere their original motive, become seized by ambition or by a pleasure in ordering others about, but so do some individualists become selfish and seized by spiritual pride ; the two ways of thought are not to be compared by comparing such men. Wise collectivists do not need to be told by their critics that collective action is often wasteful and contradictory ; they are well aware of it ; and yet they say with honest and brave conviction : there is no other way to mitigate the evils of society ; it is clumsy, we know, but we are bound to persist in it ; and they point to the good that has been done — the reform of the prison system, for example, or the organization of hospitals, or the advances that have been made towards social security — all of which, they say, has resulted from collective action. They are, therefore, impatient of those who are less interested in framing a new set of prison regulations or in extending the franchise or in raising the general standard of living than they are in learning how, within his material circumstances, whatever they are, a man may live in peace with himself and with his neighbours and with his God. To think in these terms, the collectivists say, is to think unpractically. How can a man live a life of beauty and peace who is hungry or ill-housed or without basis in security ? And how — the world being what it is — can he obtain a better house or greater security except by organizing himself in groups to demand and insist upon these things ? Surely they must come first ?

There are two replies to this : a radical reply, which cuts through the whole collectivist argument in a struggling return to first principles ; and a less drastic reply, which seeks to distinguish between good and evil groups, between a collectivism which rebounds upon itself and a collectivism which does not. The radical reply is given by Tolstoy in Nehludof's meditation in the last chapter of " Resurrection " :

In this way the idea that the only certain means of salvation from the terrible evil from which men are suffering is that they should always acknowledge themselves to be guilty before God, and therefore unable to punish or reform others, became clear to him. It became clear to him that all the dreadful evil he had been witnessing in prisons and jails, and the quiet self-assurance of the perpetrators of this evil, resulted from men's attempting what was impossible : to correct evil while themselves evil. Vicious men were trying to reform other vicious men, and thought they could do it by using mechanical means. . . . The answer he had been unable to find was the same that Christ gave to Peter. [The reference is to Matt. xviii, 21-35.] It was, to forgive always, every one, to forgive an infinite number of times, because there are none who are not themselves guilty, and therefore none who can punish or reform.

This is the supreme answer of enlightened individualism. There is none who can reform others until he himself is remade from within. But it is an answer which, in the form Tolstoy gives it, great numbers of good men, who feel that they have a vocation to the collective reformation of society, are incapable of accepting. They say, in any case, that collective action is *their* method of remaking themselves, and that the alternative to it is, for them, a stagnant resignation, an acquiescence in evil. A less drastic restatement of Tolstoy's answer must, therefore, be attempted, and it seems to be that, if any organizations are good, those are best which have as their aim not to reform men but to enable them to reform themselves, and which remain continuously aware that, in so far as their purpose is to change material conditions, their work is itself merely conditional — a means, and at best a doubtful means, never an end, and, therefore, carrying within it no kind of justification of fanaticism or coercion or violence — or, even, of collective self-righteousness. The word " enable " has appeared again.

If the work of good organizations is properly to be regarded as a permissive or enabling means, and never as an end, and if this is among the tests of the good or evil of an organization, it is necessary to ask : what is the end, the purpose external to the organization itself, which, by preserving as it were the perspective of its activities, prevents those activities from becoming corrupt and tyrannical and saves the group itself from being " an instrument of destructive fate, causing men to ' drown and kill ' one another contrary to their interest and free will " ? The end, surely, is the end of all life on earth : that man may so experience life as to feel that it is part of a glory, not the inhabiting of a prison, and, when his conditions appear to him to be those of a prison, may have power to transcend them. In this respect, life is comparable with art, and the estimation of life with the estimation of art. In the first of his " Essays on Literature and Life ", that greatly humane critic, Clutton-Brock, in speaking of the supreme passages of art, those in which Shakespeare or Beethoven or Michael Angelo " had the power of saying more than mortal things ", says that art sets us a standard " not only of making or doing things, but of being ".

For these great moments express, and actually bring about in us, a state of being different from our ordinary life, so different that we may call it transcendent. While we are in it we know that our ordinary life has purpose or value [and here is Clutton-Brock re-defining what we have called " the end "] — has purpose or value only in so far as it prepares for and leads up to these rare moments of transcendent being.

But we forget this in the routine of life. Men are absent-minded about their true desire and irrelevantly occupied with other things. It is true that we must have good drains and government and meat and drink before we can turn to our passion for the absolute . . . but the precedent conditions are only conditions, and we are always forgetting that.

It is this, above all else, that collective reformers have to remember, for, if they forget that all their work is merely conditional, their organization begins to assume in their eyes the shape of a divine purpose and their fingers begin to itch for the harp of self-righteousness or the thunder-bolts of power.

This was already clear to Tolstoy before what has been called his conversion ; he expressed it in the Second Epilogue to " War and Peace " and, indeed, by implica-tion, throughout the novel itself ; and year by year since then the events of the world have borne in its truth upon us. But men are very slow to acknowledge this truth in their own persons. They fear that to be critical of groups and organizations as such, to doubt their virtue and efficacy, is to be guilty of defeatism. Looking abroad they see how perilous groups may be, and yet, even abroad, they have been slow to recognize the peril. How many there were who, observing the material reforms effected by Fascism in its early years, excused its excesses with the parrot-cry of all tyrants — that there can be no omelette without a breaking of eggs, and who, in any case, failed to perceive that here was the very pattern of an evil organization, fanatical, coercive, an enslaver of men's free will, a law unto itself, a pursuer of conditional things as if they were final things.

The Italian evil has now declared itself ; so has the German ; and yet there are many collectivists in England and America who will not see that in the corruption of German and Italian collectivism there is a criticism of all collectivism, whatever its name. The Germans were fully entitled to organize a new system of government if it pleased them to do so, but as soon as that system became anything but an enablement and protection of individual free will, as soon as it began to insist that life had purpose or value in the ascendancy of a mass and not in the transcendence of the personal spirit, it became corrupt and an instrument of man's self-destruction. That a group is democratic in form does not exempt it from critical examination. Democracy is nothing magical; it is not the cloak of darkness or the shoes of swiftness ; it is not, in itself, virtuous ; to suppose that it is is to commit the totalitarian sin against the light. Democracy is a system of government, which has been found by certain peoples to be on the whole, and subject to important limitations, more convenient to them than other systems. The groups arising within it are as much open to criticism as groups arising within any other governmental system. They are as liable to become engrossed in solemn irrelevance, and, insisting always on the conditions of the human prison — its government and its drains, to forget that the purpose of mankind is not to improve the prison but to transcend it. " How seldom ", says Clutton-Brock, " does anyone rise in the House of Commons and, instead of speaking to the question, suddenly cry :

> Helen, thy beauty is to me
> Like those Nicean barks of yore —

to remind the other members of what they spend their lives in forgetting."

On Unrelated Knowledge

I PROPOSE, in this final essay, to state a problem which arises naturally from all that has gone before, and to abstain deliberately from offering a ready-made solution of it. There are two good reasons for thus abstaining : the first, that though I have often meditated upon the problem's nature and have, so to speak, explored that dark wood and seen light shining into it in such a way as has seemed to give a hint of its boundaries, I will by no means presume to draw a map of it; the second, that the way out is not to be won by axe and shouting or by the guidance of any one man or hard-lined policy, but will become apparent, if ever it appears, only in the retrospect of some future time. We shall find the way out, if we find it at all, by the exercise of a common patience in inquiry, by listening to the wisdom of men whose paths in the wood are different from our own, and by distrusting those who cry : " I have found it ! " For the wood is universal, a complexity of light and darkness, of aspiration and despair ; outside, we believe, is open country, an epoch that might long afterwards be spoken of as the Re-enlightenment, as we now speak of the Renaissance ; and certainly, if we come into that country, it will not be by a singly directed movement but by a general emergence, comparable in this respect with the process of the Renaissance itself. In brief, mankind will move towards the edge of the wood by divergent paths ; the ways out are not one but many ; but none will be found as long as the nature and indeed the existence of the wood go unrecognized, and men walk about in circles within it. For this reason, though the task will not be one of easy optimism and will be dissatisfying to those who have their patent medicine for all ills, it may be of value to ask what the wood is and how we came into it — or suffered it to grow up about us, and to distinguish it from the trees ; for, if the problem be but stated, other men, whose point of view is different from mine, may re-state it ; religion, science, poetry and statesmanship may converge upon it ; and so, gradually, the peoples become actively aware of it, as they are not now.

They are not actively aware, but they are aware of it. " Something is wrong ", they say, " we are in a mess, we are entangled. We have been taught for many years that the difficulties of civilization are at root economic, and, though the gaps in that argument have lately appeared to widen, we recognize its force. But the economists, whether they differ or agree, speak a language foreign to us, and not only to us, the peoples, but to experts in other branches of knowledge, so that when we listen to those who should lead us we are listening to a babel of thought and are confused. One says that all good will follow from a raising of the standard of living ; another that this is to be attained by subduing the forces of Nature ; while a third points out that though, in fact, for many years, Nature has been more and more subdued and the standard of living steadily raised, the world is in a sorry state ; subdued Nature has been directed against man, who is poor, conscribed and in hourly peril. Something is wrong, we are in a mess, we are entangled. Every promised good — the conquest of the air, for example — breeds a consuming evil ; every expediency demands a vile price — the safe-guarding of the realm from internal enemies having driven us to the imprisonment of men without trial. We have ships and aircraft but cannot go abroad ; we have universities, but may not educate our youth in the humanities.

A gigantic and paradoxical riddle, not of war only but extending far on into a victorious peace, is pressing upon us. We do not understand the thousand answers that are offered because we do not understand the question. Something is wrong, we are in a mess, we are entangled. But in what ?

This is an indication of the problem in its crudest form " Nam ipsa scientia potestas est " has lost its true meaning. Man has begun to feel that he is battered by knowledge, not empowered and liberated by it. This is not only because knowledge has been perverted in use and made destructive, but for the deeper reason that knowledge in one kind has become separated from knowledge in another, and the citizen, upon whom the effects of it are outpoured, feels himself to be an operator in a demoniacal telephone-exchange, where voices rain demands upon him in variously incomprehensible tongues and he can establish no connexions between them. This is a kind of madness, and the phrase " The world has gone mad ! " is frequently heard. Though spoken half-seriously and often in the tone of one who wishes to imply that he knows himself to be exaggerating, it is not a phrase to be disregarded. Men often exaggerate the expression of what they feel in order to hide from others and from themselves that they feel it, and it is useless to attempt to hide from ourselves that, underlying the chatter of reassurance which buzzes for a week or two about each new plan or palliative, there is a profound sense that human endeavour has become divided against itself and life disharmonized.

The first thing to understand, if the problem is to be understood at all, is that this disharmony is not caused by war and will not cease with it. It appears, on the contrary, to have its origin at least as far back as the end of the sixteenth or the beginning of the seventeenth century. John Palmer spoke, in his biography of Ben Jonson, of " the great negation " offered by Puritanism to the flowering of the English Renaissance, and, in his context, he had good reason ; but Puritanism was much more than a negation, it was a substituting of one way of life for another that had spent itself, and we fall into every kind of historical peril if we do not recognize that the force of the Renaissance was indeed spent when Ben Jonson died, and that, in spite of its abounding glories, there was one respect in which it may be said to have failed. It rested, not in England only, but throughout Europe, upon a belief that a synthesis of knowledge was possible and that such a synthesis when attained would be power with wisdom. This belief's anthropomorphous form lay in the idea of a Universal Man, all-wise because omniscient ; Leonardo and Bacon, each in his own way, aspired to omniscience and struggled for it. Universality, not specialization, was the ideal of that noble age, and even by More himself so vast an aspiration was not felt to be a challenge to the Divine omniscience, but, on the contrary, an earthly mirror of it. But, in the event, knowledge outgrew man's power to assimilate it. Early in the Renaissance the empire of a universal mind seemed not unattainable, but the frontiers ran out and out, the edge of the world receded before the passionate traveller. Before Bacon died the game was up. The limitations upon his own knowledge, his failure to grasp many of the major extensions won by the work of his contemporaries, prove it. If he failed there was little hope for others. The men of the Renaissance had by their genius so raised the stakes that a change in the rules had become imperative, and Puritanism changed them. In the year of the " Novum Organum ", itself no more than a marvellous fragment of its author's all-embracing dream, the Pilgrim Fathers landed in New England.

It seems to be one of the characteristics of Puritanism

that, where its original impulse weakens, it does not nominate its own successor. There is an interregnum and a dangerous one. Those who know most about the system of co-education in America and are most sympathetically disposed towards it say, for example, when explaining the difficulties which attend it nowadays, that it came into existence when the rules of Puritan conduct were much stronger upon the young than they now are, so that students, coming to college from Puritan homes, accepted as natural what is now a conscious act of self-denial ; and what has happened there — the gradual devitalizing of the Puritan rule without the emergence of another with an equal power to sustain individual conscience — has happened elsewhere and on far wider territory.

Since the Renaissance, knowledge has grown without intermission. Fortunately, during the seventeenth and the greater part of the eighteenth centuries, the application of knowledge did not outstrip knowledge itself. Men continued to move at about the same pace, to keep their self-multiplication within reasonable bounds, to preserve the decencies of earshot and eyeshot, to depend much upon sails and horses, which are a means of sanity, and to slaughter each other for the most part professionally. In the nineteenth century, they discovered how to apply what they knew, and applied it to acquire what the " Meditationes Sacrae " did not mean by " potestas ". At the same time, the Puritan rule, which might have set bounds to this violent appetite, became devitalized, the ideal of the Renaissance was gone long ago, and knowledge ground out its perilous abundance as the mill ground out salt in the fairy-tale. In a desire to grasp at something, men have specialized more and more. Where great minds, which in the sixteenth century might have aspired to universal knowledge, have specialized, there has been produced in them that humility, that humane and indeed holy gentleness, which, when we encounter it in men of science, we love, as being perhaps the first gleam of the Re-enlightenment, the radiance beyond the dark wood. But specialization can be also an ambuscade of charlatans and faithless men who cling to the wood for the importance that the darkness lends to their little torches, and a part of the human problem is the difficulty of distinguishing, where we are not specialists, between those who are.

The difficulty may appear to be insuperable. How, it may be asked, shall a man choose between two advisers whose science is unknown to him ? Can he do more than have regard for the repute and visible qualification of each, and blindly accept the counsel of him who has, or seems to have, the greater authority ? And yet, to do this is to abdicate, to hand over civilization to superstition and the rule of oracles. Nor is it necessary. A great Judge does not wring his hands and put off his robes and step down from the bench in the presence of expert witnesses ; even a Parliamentary committee, when a private Bill is before it, assumes that it has the right and the power to discern the public interest amid a conflict of technical evidence ; and civilization, if it is to survive, must become, and prove itself to be, capable of no less. Civilization has to learn how to be judicial, and democracy, if democracy is to continue, how to endure that responsibility of judgment which kings have accepted.

If we consider what a great Judge is and by what principles he is sustained, the nature of civilization's problem in attempting to apply those principles to itself may be made clearer. A Judge submits his human prejudice to the guidance of a rule — that of the law — which, though not immutable, is continuous from the past into the future, and, at the time of his giving judgment, is absolute upon him. Though he is not trained in the science of chemistry or engineering or electricity, he is trained in the science of relating these and all other subjects to the law. Thus he is safeguarded from the little vanity, to which the rest of us are subject, of putting his money on this expert or that, and from the weakness of being flattered by a glimmer of technical understanding into considering himself a technician ; for he knows that it is not his business to decide whether one chemist is better than another, but only how the conflicting chemical evidence is related to his overriding absolute — the law. In brief, though a man, he has put up about himself — as a priest does in the confessional — a wall against certain human frailties and passions, and has learned how to live within it.

Return now to the analogy. As a Judge is fortified by the law, so may men be fortified by their sense of values — a principle of life imperative upon them from within, overriding their appetites and fears. But to have a principle of life is not enough. As a Judge may know the law and yet be a bad Judge because he has not a judicial temper with which to apply it to particular cases, so a man may have a good principle of life and yet be a tyrannical or perverse citizen because he has not a judicial mind with which to apply that principle to controversy — a mind, that is to say, which reads facts and opinions not for their immediate consequence or for their seeming authority or for their inherent pleasingness, but always for their relationship to a continuous, though mutable, principle of life. How to encourage and make effective among civilized men this judicial mentality appears to be the constructive problem underlying all other problems of our time.

It is worth observing, in order that the problem may be seen in its historical perspective, that it is a twofold problem of self-discipline and synthesis. The answer to it would, if it were found, be an answer to the two great questions that the past has bequeathed to us : first, what self-discipline shall man impose upon himself as an alternative to the rule of Puritanism ? and, secondly, what synthesis shall he seek as an alternative to the Renaissance's ideal of omniscience ? And yet of those who speak to the mind of the world, whether in the Press or in the universities, few speak in these terms. Self-discipline — the deliberate recognition by man of his frailties and limitations in order that, by purging the human claim of its impossibilities, its reasonable hope may be made less improbable — is little taught. We, who have not the personal confidence of the seventeenth century, have instead a collective and profane arrogance which pretends that men can do what man cannot. At the same time, having abandoned hope of a single omniscience, we have pressed out, radially, to the opposite extreme of vocational education ; and a profound study of the humane letters, from which arises an understanding of the relationship of things, is seldom recognized as being what it is — a crying practical necessity of the modern world, for without it there will be for ever a multitude of witnesses but no Judge.

This is the black heart of the problem — the Court of Civilization is without a Judge, and still the specialists bring up more and more cases for hearing. Men are still being taught that hope lies in an indiscriminate multiplying of their wants and in subduing Nature to the satisfaction of them ; seldom that the remedy against chaos is in selection, which implies renouncement, and in synthesis. For the same reason — that of flattering a sick materialism — men are asked to believe that their problem is external to themselves, organizational not spiritual, and that Utopia can be built upon what they desire and do, independently of what they are. But against that belief they are beginning to rebel. Whoever

224

will say fearlessly that materialism is sick unto death, that there are no more scapegoats, and that the peoples must learn how to judge before their decisions can be valid, has his audience to-day among the young of England and America. They have begun to distrust unrelated knowledge. Though they have not a map of the wood, they feel its darkness about them, and are becoming less and less gullible by the little guides with torches. They are in a mood, if the great universities will but go with them, to cast back to the first principles of judgment.

THE END